JUBILEE JOURNEY

Hope from Now to Eternity

Kay Bascom

Olive Press
צהר זית

Jubilee Journey

Hope from Now to Eternity

Kay Bascom

JUBILEE JOURNEY *Hope from Now to Eternity*

Copyright © 2021 by Kay Bascom

Printed in the USA

ISBN 978-1-941173-48-0

Published by

Olive **P**ress Messianic and Christian Publisher
www.olivepresspublisher.org
olivepressbooks@gmail.com

צהר זית

Front cover image: "Come; for all things are ready" (Luke 14:17) was photographed for *Decision* magazine by Bud Meyer © 1967 *Decision.* Used by permission.

Back cover background textile image, Pixabay.com, public domain.

The Jubilee emblem on the back cover was sewn by Ginger Olson onto the author's grandfather's napkin. The tiny gold cross inside the star of David was a gift to the author from a faithful-to-Jesus friend, as the friend was dying.

Our prayer at Olive Press is that we may help make the Word of Adonai fully known, that it spread rapidly and be glorified everywhere. We hope our books help open people's eyes so they will turn from darkness to Light and from the power of the adversary to God and to trust in ישׁוע Yeshua (Jesus). (From II Thess. 3:1; Col. 1:25; Acts 26:18,15 NRSV *New Revised Standard Version* and CJB, the Complete Jewish Bible.)

All Scriptures, unless otherwise indicated, are taken from THE HOLY BIBLE, NEW INTERNATIONAL VERSION®, NIV®. Copyright © 1973, 1978, 1984 by International Bible Society. Used by permission of Zondervan Publishing House. All rights reserved, worldwide.

(Note that the later 2011 revision is what most online and app versions are, but the author uses her own 1984 print copy.)

Scriptures marked RSV are taken from the *Revised Standard Version* of the Bible, copyright © 1946, 1952, and 1971 the Division of Christian Education of the National Council of the Churches of Christ in the United States of America.

Our personal jubilees
are like dress rehearsals
before the curtain on
eternity rises.

OTHER BOOKS BY THE AUTHOR:

THE MESSIAH MYSTERY: The Old and New Testaments' Inseparable Disclosure

KEYS TO MESSIAH MYSTERY, a study guide

ALL: He fulfilled all, He deserves our all

IN: Messiah in me, and I in Him

THEREFORE: When truth is proclaimed, action is required

HIDDEN TRIUMPH IN ETHIOPIA

OVERCOMERS

OVERCOMERS STUDY GUIDE (for then and now)

(See page 190 and olivepresspublisher.com for more information.)

TABLE OF CONTENTS

BEFORE YOU BEGIN READING....

An eclectic mix: Dear Reader, please have patience with this book's interweaving of biblical content and personal vignettes that cross back and forth over time and space. Hopefully, our attempts to apply God's directives to our own family's life may encourage others in creative experimentation with life's jubilees. My intentionally panoramic way of exploring God's truth is meant to encourage that invaluable sort of study as it moves toward the happy expectation of God's great Jubilee.

Bold headings: These section titles throughout each chapter serve to break the text into digestible portions and hopefully help the reader identify variegated strands of thought being woven together.

Response pages: Each chapter's response page gives an opportunity for the reader to rethink the chapter's content and consider how it might be personally applied. Those pages could also serve as discussion material if two or more people study the book together.

Verse references: Why are so many verse references given? The author sees Scripture as God's truth and is concerned about stating what is scripturally correct. "Bereans" are commended for searching the Scriptures, "to see if these things be so" (Acts 17:11). References help the readers check sources and draw their own conclusions.

Divine names: "LORD" in capital letters is most translations' rendering of the divine name for Jehovah (Yahweh, YHWH), distinguishing it from another divine name in Hebrew, Adonai, rendered "Lord" in small letters. Occasionally the name *Yeshua* is used for Jesus, to remind us of the Savior's Jewish context.

Translations and capitalization inconsistencies: Verse references herein are largely from the NIV translation. Like most versions of the Bible, the NIV does not capitalize pronouns for deity. When I write, however, it seems fitting for me to capitalize them. Therefore, "His" and "He" appear repeatedly in the text, although when the Bible is quoted directly, capitals do not appear.

"Author's emphasis added": I'm assuming the reader will realize that my italics or underlining in the midst of a quotation are my attempt to highlight a specific word or phrase, and were not in the original.

INTRODUCTION

Dear reader, you may understand this book better if I explain its mode and progression. Most readers today would have little interest in exploring the biblical Jubilee proclaimed in Leviticus 25. It would seem out of date and its application limited to a foreign culture of long ago. The Bible, however, is a document that stretches across time in one way, and is "timeless" in another. Biblical revelation begins with sort of a "picture book" for Israel, the community the Creator was guiding into their role as the Messianic family. They were to bring forth the Son who would defeat sin and death, and provide salvation for fallen humanity.

God's Word provides a whole array of pictures, object lessons, and worded guidance. The "feasts unto the Lord" (at the close of which the Jubilee appears) is just one of the Master Teacher's ways to reveal Himself to the world He loves so deeply as to ordain a plan of reconciliation between Himself and us. Watching Him reveal His heart through the Jubilee lens can take us on an interwoven journey. It moves through foreshadows in the Old Testament books...to the New Testament fulfillments in the arrival of the Jubilee's ultimate Kinsman Redeemer, Jesus... and even on to the ultimate Jubilee when eternity begins.

This book also progresses through my extended Jubilee journey, both through the Scriptures and through my own life. The Bible is like a mirror through which we see reflections of our Lord, but we also see ourselves—how we are implicated, included, and mercifully invited into God's family. In the process of writing this—and with the overlay of the Coronavirus pandemic of 2020—my own Jubilee understandings and applications to life have grown. I trust that the book's exploration can awaken your interest in what God keeps saying to us, in so many ways. The book of Hebrews puts the progression of God's revelation clearly:

> In the past God spoke to our forefathers through the prophets at many times and in various ways, but in these last days he has spoken to us by his Son, whom he appointed heir of all things, and through whom he made the universe (Hebrews 1:1-2).

That Son is who the Jubilee leads us to, the Redeemer provided for the world. As musician Michael Card's song expresses it so beautifully, "Jesus is our Jubilee."

Chapter 1
CATALYST

To be honest, I had never liked the term "Jubilee." To me, the concept sounded sort of unrealistic, or overstated. I couldn't picture it in any context I welcomed, and I had no idea how much it meant to the God who ordained its fulfillment. My changed appraisal of the Jubilee idea came as a surprise. This new orientation to its meaning began in East Africa decades ago, and has continued right up to now.

But why should a reader care how I've been processing a single word? I wouldn't have thought it worth my time to write this if I hadn't eventually discovered that the wealth of the Jubilee was eminently worth sharing. It was meant to be communal, so how could I keep it to myself?

Most readers like take-aways. If you'll join me on this journey, I'm trusting that you will find it personally valuable on a number of levels. Its many facets include deepened biblical understanding, fascinating life enrichments, encouragement in difficult times, and a growing grasp of God's overall goal of restoration. Although the Jubilee search begins with how the LORD organized His people when He gave them the Torah (the Mosaic law), its principles are valuable in any generation, and its foreshadowing is fascinating to trace right up to today, and on into the future.

DOUBLE RELEVANCE

All of us are living between our Jubilees. God's Jubilee pattern has to do with the corporate life experience of His people, and with the individual as well. The Jubilee year was the fiftieth, the year to be approached through an intentional process. Most of us get to a fiftieth in our own lives, but we may not be preparing for it. And looking ahead, we will each either ignore or embrace God's final Jubilee, the ultimate celebration of reconciliation. Wherever you are along your micro timeline or His macro timeline, discovering the Jubilee's keys to a good life can bless the path of your own pilgrimage. Discerning life's deepest meanings should not be left untended, and the Owner's Manual provides vital keys to discovery, and recovery as well.

How did I happen to get into this odd arena of study and life application? An experience years ago inspired my curiosity and became the catalyst. Let me set the scene of the event that introduced me to this mystery to which I had given no previous thought. But first, I need to explain the trauma that drew me into caring.

REVOLUTION

Just prior to my introduction to the Jubilee, our family was caught in the midst of on-the-ground experiments in theories of government. Having begun to serve in medical missions in Ethiopia in the 1960s in the Horn of Africa, we were deeply impacted by the abrupt and violent change of government Ethiopia experienced when their centuries-old monarchial form of government was overturned in the 1970's by a Marxist coup. Ethiopia's King Haile Selassie had won the world's respect during the Italian invasion of Ethiopia preceding the second World War. The Emperor brought his nation into modernity with remarkable skill. Yet in his aging years, his perpetual lack of dealing with serfdom and land reform sparked fervor in Ethiopia's youth. The very students whom the Emperor had spearheaded into modern education dreamed of changes that were not happening. Ironically, their restlessness became the fulcrum of the Emperor's undoing. The vacuum of his inaction set the stage for students to buy into the Marxist diagnosis and cure.

When the Emperor was deposed in 1974, Ethiopia became what one author titled his book, "The Country that Cut off its Head." In 1977, various young communist groups were competing for which would be the most doctrinaire, the most "red." This bred a reign of killings, known as "the Red Terror," throughout Addis Ababa, Ethiopia's capital city. The new Marxist government confiscated all mission hospitals, clinics, and schools, and confined missionaries to the capital. Among hundreds of other Westerners branded as "Imperialists," we were propelled out of the country to wherever we might land. For Ethiopia's mission communities, the nearest place we could get our teens into schooling was the Rift Valley Academy in neighboring Kenya.

EAST AFRICAN INFERNO

Spun out of the land and people we loved, we found ourselves stuck in Nairobi, Kenya, treading water along with assorted refugees. Expatriate missionary, business, and diplomatic personnel, as well as citizens at risk, had been cast out of their various locations by East Africa's wider turmoil. Hungry nationals from bordering Uganda walked the streets, having fled from the horrors of Idi Amin, their country's demented dictator bent on Islamizing his kingdom at any cost. Neighboring Ethiopia and Somalia repeatedly clashed over the Ogaden area. On Kenya's northern border, a shaky peace accord had recently quelled the civil war between Sudan's two regions, one Muslim (in the north), and the other made up of subjugated animists and Christians (in the south).

RESPITE

Mercifully, Rift Valley Academy agreed to take our group of teenagers, whose school in Ethiopia had been confiscated for the Marxist government's use. Our two younger sons were therefore a couple driving hours outside of Nairobi, and we didn't have a car. We parents were moving from guest house to guest house in the capital, pondering over where to go next. Even getting visas or work permits in other East African countries took time. "Visa any day," they would say, as the months ticked by.

My dear husband, Doctor Charlie, and I found ourselves idle and trying to make sense of the suffering and displacements experienced by fellow street walkers who had fled various totalitarian East African regimes. One day, when downtown taking Arabic lessons, our curiosity was piqued by a placard advertising lectures on "Christianity and Ideologies," being presented by a British chemist serving as a Nairobi pastor, and a Cornell-trained agricultural economist.

SHOCK!

Exiting the Center's elevator the next week, we filed into a lecture hall with about 100 people who resembled a UN assembly of various nationalities and races. The lecturers were handing out stapled 8 X 14 inch notes. Both men were expatriate residents in Kenya. To the Kenyan and foreign listeners who had been caught in the crux of governance upheavals, their weekly presentations were electric. Their analysis of the systems from which some of us had been ousted brought forth questions from the audience, shouts of agreement, or angry objections.

Being hooked and hungry for answers, each week we listened intently and studied the meaty handouts that examined three classic forms of government. These weren't theoretical high school civics lectures; they were sophisticated dissections of Socialism, Marxism, and Capitalism. With East Africa thrashing around in the throes of these political whirlwinds, Kenya was the one stable nation right in the eye of the storm. When would Kenya be swept into the carnage? South of Nairobi lay Tanzania's socialistic experiment. Up north, Ethiopia's communist revolution raged. To the west and north, Islam was wreaking havoc on non-Muslims. Meanwhile, Kenya was still smarting over its former British capitalist colonization. The lecturers' arguments brought forth passionate outbursts from a socialist devotee here, or a Marxist functionary there, while Kenyans listened attentively.

But what was the lecturers' ultimate purpose in all these clarifications and refutations? To our utter amazement, nearing the end of the series, their actual purpose came out. In light of the examined weaknesses and tyrannies of socialism, communism, and capitalism, all three, what was a wise nation to choose? What principles of governance were they proposing Kenya embrace? Their seventh lecture, "The Social, Political, and Economic System of the Old Testament Law" presented principles set up by the One who best knows the heart of man. The eighth and last lecture, "Reform or Revolution," presented the alternative of a divine perspective on socio-economic change.

Wonder of wonders, these astute lecturers surprised the audience by the audacity of suggesting a prescription for overcoming the compounding evils a society faces in a fallen world. And where might we find an antidote that humanity would need to neutralize or reduce our suffering? Enter God's prescription, in which the Jubilee provisions in Leviticus 25 play a significant role. Yes, they turned to God's pattern of periodic re-calibrations prescribed in His "Owner's Manual."

THE METANARRATIVE

At that point, immersed in the fall-out of national disasters arising out of various political theories, my focus was on East Africa—immediate and visceral. Only much later did I rethink why the lecturers' recommendation actually spoke to the universal human condition. Leviticus' societal principles arose out of our Creator's understanding of fallen humanity's selfishness, greed, and tendency to oppress each other. Man is in bondage to these sins and needs a way to be freed. We wonder, "How can injustices be put right, and healthy relationships be restored?"

RELEVANT THEN... BUT NOW?

Before we turn to the Leviticus period in biblical history, dear Reader, it would be prudent to set that amazing chapter in its context to better understand how it might apply to Kenya's governance theory, or that of any nation. One might immediately argue that something given to the Hebrews over 3,000 years ago could hardly be useful to a modern nation today.

Not so fast. Keep the question in its full context—meaning the history of the world. Let's consider the Genesis account of our forebears' original disastrous agreement with God's sly enemy: "Did God really say...?" (Genesis 3:1). Doubt, dysfunction, and depravity grew exponentially, as recorded in Genesis. God set a plan of redemption into action, choosing a man named Abraham to become the head of a family whose seed (singular) God said was eventually to bless the whole world. Strangely, the possession of Abraham's destined homeland, although promised, was to be delayed 400 years (Genesis 15:13).

Fast forward to Israel's bondage in Egypt, and God's miraculous deliverance from death through applying the blood of the Passover lamb on the night of their Exodus. By then Abraham's family had multiplied from seventy to thousands who had been living in slavery for centuries. God deposited their helpless community into the impossible landscape of a dry and barren desert. Their taskmasters, homes, provisions, labors, and seasonal rhythms were all gone. What now?

RECALIBRATION!

God had them right where He wanted them—with a clean slate and no distractions. He placed a symbol of His presence at the heart of the community in the Tabernacle that He carefully described, provided for, and brought into actuality. He revealed to this helpless multitude His amazing plan—who would lead them, how they would survive, what they would eat, what they would do with their time, and how their society would be harmoniously ordered.

THE MIRACLE OF WRITING

God had Moses write down in the Torah the history of His dealings with Israel and His ordained guidelines for their fledgling nation. Actually, we take for granted the amazing gift God provided to humanity through writing—that simply from letters on stone, animal skin, papyrus or paper, people can know what happened and what folks were thinking in centuries before our own times.

PAGEANTRY

Writing is not the only way ideas are transferred over centuries. Visible celebrations are powerful mechanisms harnessed to the advantage of less literate societies. In Ethiopia we had been awed by the most impressive holiday extravaganza we'd ever witnessed, the Ethiopian Orthodox Church's *Timket* parade in Addis Ababa. All over the country, similar enactments were being witnessed on January 19th.

Timket commemorates Jesus' baptism. Projected from that milestone in First Century AD, the Orthodox Christian clergy each year re-baptizes its faithful all over the country on that day. The annual procession down the streets of Addis Ababa harken back to biblical days. *Hundreds of turbaned priests in white robes, their replicas of the Ark of the Covenant hoisted above each head. Umbrellas of brilliant crimson, green, and black, trimmed in gold. Davidic actors dancing before the Ark.* Pageants are typically based on historical events, yet *Timket* seemed to us to be considerably embroidered, contextualized, and harnessed to the Church's authority. As a cultural artifact, it was simply magnificent, but I asked myself, *"Does this take liberties and assume new meanings which the written Word of God does not allow?"*

"AFRICAN ZION"

When we arrived in Ethiopia, our expectation was focused on bringing benefits of modern medicine to an African society. What we didn't expect to find was a deeply Jewish cultural experience expressed through religious practices, yet contemporary with our own Twentieth Century presence. Their calendar, their diet, and their pageantry were all curiously based on historical milestones that stretched from the 900s BC in King Solomon's time... through the Ethiopian Eunuch's conversion in the First Century AD... to the nation's Christianization under King Ezana in the Fourth Century (before Constantine)... to King Lalibela's underground churches (created for an Ethiopian pilgrimage destination mirroring the Holy Land) in the Twelfth Century... to Ethiopian Orthodox Christians still making pilgrimages to Jerusalem in the Twentieth Century. We didn't expect the traces of biblical history that we began recognizing over the realm—towns named Nazareth, women named Bet-le-ham, the Capitol's Ghion Hotel. Furthermore, up north lived a mysterious community of Black Jews who traced their history to pre-Christian times, and who still sacrificed lambs at Easter.

Ethiopia is called the "African Zion." To us, history seemed compressed there, although historical actualities appeared to be re-interpreted and manipulated in ways that created a fascinating national epic. Repeatedly we felt the need to consult the Bible to determine accuracies or discover deviations from historical origins. All of which is just to say that one of the surprising experiences of living in Ethiopia was to be thrust back into biblical history in a perpetually living way. This challenged us to update our own application of biblical principles in line with Truth as preserved in the Scriptures.

LET'S EXPLORE!

When pushed out of Ethiopia and landing in Kenya, a new biblical connection strangely emerged: the Brits' challenge to take the Torah's principles seriously. In the next chapter, dear Reader, let's go to the Bible to try to get a feel for how our Creator thinks about time, place, relationships, and the redemptions necessitated by the predicaments of fallen humanity—elements of Jubilee "recalibration." Human nature hasn't changed since Adam and Eve. We share the same problems and can be rescued by the same divine Guide. It will be worth it to us to explore possibilities. This may involve creativity, but after all, Genesis tells us we're "made in the image of God"—the original Creator!

1 CATALYST:
How our Jubilee adventure began. Might it start yours?

✎ What does "Jubilee" bring to your mind? Why?

✎ Reading through Leviticus 25, what thoughts or questions arise?

✎ What relationship between God and the Israelites do you sense from Leviticus 25:1-2, 17, 38, 43, 55?

Chapter 2

CLUES, CODES, AND EXPERIMENTS

A dmittedly, many would be skeptical about Leviticus being relevant for our lives today. In fact, a large swath of Christendom pays little attention to Old Testament teachings at all, and concurrently, are rather blind to God's dealings with the Abrahamic family through whom He chose to bring salvation to the fallen world that John 3:16 says He "so loved."

In a drama, one needs both Act I and Act II to appreciate the story's plot and its resolution. Ignoring Act 1 of the Bible leaves us hanging in air with no foundation. History is progressive. Even today, pride in what modern civilization "knows" can cause us to forget or discount history's predecessors on whose shoulders today's culture stands. Likewise, our grappling with the relevance of the Jubilee needs to be grounded on its Old Testament meanings (Act I), before we can explore its outworking during New Testament times (Act II).

HUMANITY'S STORY

Understanding the opening chapters of a story is essential. Of course, if the author never published the book, no one could conceive of the story. But God did put His in writing. How else could we know what happened, and who thought or did what, centuries ago? But we do. The Creator tells us humanity's story—from His creation... to our fall... to His plan to redeem us... to its step-by-step outworking... to its execution... its proclamation... and its conclusion.

THE MYSTERY OF "TIME"

God provided for the measurement and very concept of time—day and night, seasons, moons—all carefully timed to a lunar calendar. Creation enshrined His "base number" for the measurement of "time" in the finite world. How? By sevens.

Consider:

Seven days of creation

Seven days in a week

Seventh day Sabbath

Seven yearly feasts unto the Lord

Seventh year rest for the land

Seven years times seven, plus one: Jubilee

Seven letters in Revelation

Seven thunders, bowls, and trumpets in Revelation

And more!

REORGANIZATION

When God delivered His community out of captivity to Pharaoh's schedule and rule, He completely reorganized and recalibrated their lives before they were allowed to enter the land that He promised them. Once out of Egypt and into the Sinai desert, He placed the symbols of His presence in the heart of their camp in the Tabernacle He had them create. He ordered their twelve tribes' arrangements, duties, and their chain of command. He set up their calendar, doubled manna on the sixth day and instructed them not to gather any on the Sabbath of their week. He provided for other occasions to rest and to trust Him for their food by not planting crops every seventh year, nor the fiftieth year of the Jubilee. He punctuated their calendar with rest times and celebratory times, all based on sevens. (Seven feasts in the year; seven times seven years culminated in the Jubilee. 7X7+1=50. Two Jubilees in a century.) Only God could have devised a plan perfectly synchronizing the moons and seasons with life's cycles.

TIME CODES

God gave the Hebrews a new calendar at Mount Sinai. He told Moses and Aaron, "This month is to be for you the first month, the first month of your year." (Exodus 12:2) They began their new life in freedom by celebrating the Passover, so they would keep remembering that the death angel passed over their homes which were marked by the blood of their sacrificial lambs, the night of their exodus out of Egypt.

If we overlook God's careful timings, we miss His codes for meaning that are revealed by God's feasts. Consider Scripture's code-revealing account in Joshua 4 and 5. Forty years after the law was given at Mount Sinai, God directed the Israelites to cross over Jordan and arrive in the Promised Land on an exact day—the 10th of Nissan. That date has served as the code for all their generations—the day the lamb is chosen, four days before the Passover. The same date "spoke" when Jesus became the final sacrificial Lamb, coming to the Temple on the 10th of Nissan, four days before His crucifixion.

SEVEN FEASTS

We need to notice that the feasts were gifts from God. They were called "feasts unto the Lord" because they called the Israelites to fellowship with Him. "These are my appointed feasts, the appointed feasts of the LORD, which you are to proclaim as sacred assemblies" (Leviticus 23:2). "Three times a year you are to celebrate a festival to me" (Exodus 23:14).

These three seasonal feast times were scheduled during the first seven months of their year. They are described in Exodus 12 and 23, Leviticus 23 and 25, Numbers 29, and Deuteronomy 16. Spring Feasts were Passover, Unleavened Bread, and First Fruits, celebrated in one sequence. Then after 50 days came the one-day Feast of Weeks. Fall feasts were another triplet celebrated consecutively: Trumpets, Day of Atonement (a fast), and the Feast of Tabernacles (or Booths). This yearly series multiplied by seven brought the community to their forty-ninth year. God's command: "Consecrate the fiftieth year and proclaim liberty throughout the land to all its inhabitants. It shall be a jubilee for you...." (Leviticus 25:10-11).

OUR CLUES BUILT OVER TIME

When Charles and I were in our twenties, we began searching for what God says in His Word about life. We had each just discovered Jesus to be alive, knowable, and had accepted Him for Who He claimed to be. That gave us a hunger to know all we could about Him, which also involved studying to understand His community and the Jewish culture at the time of His Incarnation. Eventually, our years in Ethiopia stretched our historical understanding. Our Kenyan chapter nudged us to look at salvation history in a more world-wide panoramic way. On the way home from East Africa once, in 1988, two priceless weeks in the Holy Land brought alive Israel's geography, history, and culture in dirt-and-stone and flesh-and-blood reality. Our ongoing Old Testament Bible reading kept informing our understanding of the cultural milieu in which our Savior's life on earth was imbedded. The New Testament Gospel accounts quote Old Testament history and God's fulfillment of prophecies over and over again. Jesus used the immediacy of attention afforded at a feast to call Israel to Himself, to their Messiah. Grasping the atmosphere, practices, and meanings of feast celebrations recorded in the Bible opens up deepened understanding of Jesus' incarnational sojourn on earth.

EXPERIMENTS BACK IN KANSAS

After two years in Sudan, during which our oldest son took a break from college and joined us, we five reluctantly left East Africa to get the guys situated in their next educational tracks. We settled in their grandparents' home area in Kansas, and soon bonded with a group of friends that came to be called "Wellspring Fellowship." This kinship continued after we had worked together sponsoring a L'Abri Conference at our university in 1982. Wellspring is in its fourth decade by now. Since our city hosts a university and is near a military fort, people come and go randomly. Over the years, scores of students and soldiers who had participated in Wellspring fanned out to their careers or next duty stations. Meanwhile a few families stayed put. Our activities clustered around the Swihart family's "base camp" farm area outside of town, a great place to meet for fellowship and Bible study regularly, and to occasionally host family camps and weekend conferences.

A NEW RESOURCE

Soon after we moved to Kansas, Charlie and I came across a book by Martha Zimmerman titled *Celebrate the Feasts of the Old Testament in your own home or church*. A quote on the back cover caught our interest:

> The great religious feasts as described in the Old Testament and Jewish tradition are full of spiritual truth presented in the New Testament. When those festivals are re-enacted in the Christian home, children have a living picture of Bible principles. They learn far better by experiencing than by only hearing.

This book explained the significance of each feast, provided materials and visuals to use for its observance, and gave details on "how to celebrate." The whole idea inspired experimentation that brought the feasts alive for our Wellspring community, especially the children. Following the injunctions in Leviticus 23, and encouraged by Martha's book, we tried out celebrations. The kids loved building a *sukkah* at the fall Feast of Tabernacles and decorating its latticed roof with fruits and vegetables. Learning about *Tashlich* by throwing pebbles (representing our sins) into the creek on *Rosh Hashanah* was a favorite.

Wellspring hosted a couple Seder suppers at our church, later at another church, and one at our university's International Student Center. These "immersions" helped us to identify with the Hebrews' exodus out of slavery in Egypt and to get a feel for the Jewish community's annual Passover remembrance. When possible, we asked Messianic Jews—who believe Jesus truly was and is their Messiah—to lead those services. They were well-equipped to explain how the Seder foods and text amazingly point to the coming Messiah, deepening each element's meaning for believers in Jesus.

WHAT MIGHT A JEWISH SABBATH FEEL LIKE?

During this time in our lives, our three sons, then in college, often brought home classmates for weekend visits. Having our dear guys to ourselves was becoming infrequent. One Thanksgiving when they didn't bring home company, we five agreed to try something new. Knowing the Sabbath to be the basic "feast" from which the others emanated, how about trying a Sabbath ourselves? Church goers keep busy on Sundays, so their supposed "day of rest" is quite different from a Jewish Sabbath. Using Martha Zimmerman's text on how Gentiles could celebrate Jewish feasts, we experimented with the Sabbath chapter as best we could figure out.

We disconnected from the world of phones and visitors, and strung a rope across our country home's gravel driveway saying "Engaged, come another time please." The grandmother who lived with us cross-stitched a special Sabbath *challah* bread plate cover and the grandmother who lived in town spent Friday night with us, so as to keep us all sealed in.

We watched the sky for the two stars announcing the Sabbath. To begin the Sabbath supper, the mother was to light the two candles representing Creation and Redemption. We said the prescribed blessings, and enjoyed a left-over-from-Thanksgiving easily prepared meal. The Sabbath was spent leisurely, some taking their sack lunches to the upper pasture. Some studied Scripture, some took naps. Candlelight and another ceremonial meal closed the day. The peaceful lack of interruption and leisurely focus on the deeper things of life in just those twenty-four hours from sunset Friday to sunset Saturday proved to be a remarkably restful and treasured family object lesson. It was hard to explain how uniquely we felt bathed in tangible rest and freedom. We were all loath to relinquish that day's gift of a Jewish Sabbath.

PERMISSION?

One might ask, "Should Gentiles celebrate the Jewish feasts, try Sabbaths, eat Passover Seders, build booths?" In the habit of using Scripture as our guide, we based our celebrations on New Testament passages (nearly all written by Jews) telling us that believing Gentiles are grafted into their Jewish root. The early church was nearly all Jewish, but God revealed that in trusting the promised Seed for their salvation, Gentiles are adopted into the covenant community. Therefore, we feel a closeness and permission that the unbelieving Jewish community might not understand. Messianic Jews sometimes lead Gentiles in celebrations of the Passover in order to show us its fulfillment in the Lord Jesus Christ. Attending the Passover Seder with Jewish friends in our local Synagogue has been another "enricher" and expression of solidarity with the community to whom Christians owe their very existence. As Paul wrote,

> Theirs is the adoption as sons; theirs is the divine glory, the covenants, the receiving of the law, the temple worship and the promises. Theirs are the patriarchs, and from them is traced the human ancestry of Christ, who is God over all, forever praised! Amen (Romans 9:4-5).

Writing to Gentile believers in Jesus, Paul explains, "He redeemed us in order that the blessing given to Abraham might come to the Gentiles through Christ Jesus" (Galatians 3:14).

BUT OUR EXPERIMENTS WITH FEASTS MISSED THEIR CLIMAX!

The Jubilee of Leviticus 25 was actually a feast aspect we overlooked during these Wellspring experiments, which were based largely on Leviticus 23 and cross-references. It was our looming fiftieth wedding anniversary that sparked my interest in the 25th chapter of Leviticus that outlines the Jubilee. Blindness to the personal relevance of one's 50th year may be natural, since today's is a "now" culture. We don't tend to think ahead to our fiftieth birthday; in fact, we may avoid its implications. Even a fiftieth wedding anniversary may be threatening. And after all, these occasions only happen once on the calendar of most lifetimes.

Chapter 4 will relate how Jubilee exploration impacted our own fiftieth year of marriage. But first, it is important to give thought to how the Old Testament and the New Testament work together. Meshing them doubles their levels of meaning. These are connections that the Spirit of God would not want us to miss.

2 CLUES, CODES, and EXPERIMENTS: Feasts' functions and how we tried them

✎ From Exodus 23:14-19, list the three feast seasons. (From Leviticus 25, notice a fuller description that includes all 7 feasts, showing triple ones in spring and fall.)

✎ Have you celebrated any of these feasts, and if so, which? What was your take-away?

✎ Which of the first five books of the Old Testament (the Torah) have you studied?

✎ What Old Testament stories do you most remember?

Chapter 3

ONE HOUSE, TWO STORIES

W e might wonder, "What does an Old Testament ordinance like the Jubilee have to teach us now? Does Jubilee play any role in New Testament times? Did Jesus ever talk about it? Should we be studying it now, or trying to apply it?"

A few segments of Christendom would almost dismiss the Old Testament, thinking it's been "superseded." This nearsighted theology wipes out three-fourths of the Bible's revealed truth, leaving a modern Christian foundationless, and in a sense, biblically illiterate. Not understanding the unity of the two covenants has led to tragic interactions between Christians and Jews over the centuries. The biblical attitude toward the two communities is deeply respectful, intertwined, and successive. We need to see the complementary unity of God's covenants, collating them. Thoroughly biblical doctrine leads to godly relationships.

TWO FLOORS OF ONE HOME

The Old and New Testaments could be pictured as the first and second floors of the same home. The lower story is the foundational floor from which the upper story rises. Either one is incomplete without the other. If the foundation is missing, the upper structure has no firm base. If the upper floor is missing, there's no shared covering. Either one alone stands exposed "without a roof." The roof points to God's eternal purpose displayed in its full glory.

Grasping the historical and theological movement from the Abrahamic and Mosaic covenants to the New Covenant opens up comparisons and contrasts. It undergirds our confidence that the process was always in God's eternal plan as He was progressively working out His redemptive purposes.

BI-CULTURAL AND BI-COVENANTAL

We can't fully experience God's message without becoming bi-cultural—knowing our own and the Hebrew culture. Becoming conversant in the history, language, and culture of the Jewish people equips us to grasp scriptural meanings in a far deeper way. God progressively revealed His truth and mysteries in layer after layer of clues, pictures, weavings, symbols, "types," ceremonies, and analogies—like the Jubilee.

When we say the Messiah *fulfilled* the Old Testament, we must not think we should dispense with the past. To deeply understand what the Messiah fulfilled, we must know from the Old Testament who He was foreshadowed to be, and what He was predicted to do. Our New Testament understanding must be *filled full* by the Old.

Thinking of a house with two floors (two covenants), some beams could run from bottom to top. Feasts teachings are like that. They appear from the Torah's foundation right on up to Jesus' fulfillment and even the future.

FEASTS' CONTINUITY
THROUGH BOTH TESTAMENTS

The Old Testament's Torah teachings provide the foundation of the house of faith. Built upon God's earliest interactions with His Creation, the Spirit's revelation progresses, history plays out, results are revealed, deeper meanings emerge, and fulfillments appear. God appoints the feasts and then uses them in a multitude of ways.

Feasts can be viewed on a number of levels. On the physical or natural level, they proceed through the Hebrew year according to the agricultural cycles of planting, growing, and harvesting, with celebrations in real time. On an historical level, the three main feast seasons memorialized God's deliverance out of Egypt (Passover), the giving of the Law on Mount Sinai (Feast of Weeks), and their sojourn in the wilderness (Feast of Booths). On a spiritual level, they represented God's relationship with His people as their Deliverer, Sustainer, and Redeemer. On a prophetic level, the feasts reveal a study in eschatology, looking to the future. Since three of the seven feasts were fulfilled together during the Savior's Passion week, and the fourth at Pentecost, it is reasonable to expect the last three also to be fulfilled together in the future.

JESUS ANNOUNCES HIS IDENTITY,
QUOTING ISAIAH

In the Old Testament, feasts appear throughout Israel's celebrations, history, and prophecies. Then when the Lord Jesus appears on earth in the Incarnation, He introduces Himself in the synagogue in Nazareth on the basis of a prophetic reference. Unrolling the scroll of Isaiah to what is now called the 61st chapter, He stuns the congregation by reading this proclamation, and applying it to Himself:

> The Spirit of the Lord is on me, because he has anointed me to preach good news to the poor. He has sent me to proclaim freedom for the prisoners and recovery of sight for the blind, the release of the oppressed, to proclaim the year of the Lord's favor (Luke 4:18-19).

Sitting down, He says to the stunned crowd, "Today this scripture is fulfilled in your hearing." God's proclamation in Leviticus 25:10 had called the Jubilee the year to proclaim liberty throughout the land. That day in Nazareth, God-in-Christ was using code language, prophetic language. His community would have understood the implications, while we today could completely miss the shock of His proclamation. His meaning was not lost on them, for they tried to throw Him over a cliff.

JESUS REVEALED HIS IDENTITY AT FEASTS

Throughout the Lord's three-year ministry, much occurs in the context of those years' feasts—times when thousands gathered to celebrate in Jerusalem. If we don't know their background, we can't envision the backdrop of these ceremonies or feel the electricity of these encounters. Hayyim Schauss, in his book. *The Jewish Festivals,* describes Jesus' interaction with the customary water ceremony during the Feast of Tabernacles. At the dramatic completion of the water pouring ceremony (representative of the Holy Spirit), Jesus' voice echoes throughout the Temple: "If any man thirst, let him come unto me and drink. Whoever believes in me, as the Scripture has said, streams of living water will flow from within him" (John 7:37-38).

No wonder that after this incident, the officers went back to the chief priests, saying, "No one ever spoke the way this man does" (John 7:46). But that was not all. Jesus used the circumstances of that feast as a dramatic platform for revealing His identity in the night ceremonies, as well. Hayyim Schauss (page 183-184) constructs the scene at the moment of another of Jesus' astounding proclamations at the customary Torch Dance around the burning menorah lights:

> Evening has come. The great Court of the Women is crowded with people, ready for the celebration.... In the center of the court burn great golden menorahs, set on bases.... Each menorah has four branches, which terminate in huge cups into which oil is poured. Four ladders are placed against each menorah and four young priests mount them and pour oil into the cups to keep the wicks burning (wicks were made from the worn-out garments of the priests). The light of these menorahs attains such intensity that all Jerusalem is lit up by them. The lights flare up, higher and still higher, the sound of flutes is heard....

We can only imagine the impact of Jesus' loud voice calling out in such a setting, "I am the light of the world; he who follows me will not walk in darkness, but will have the light of life" (John 8:12). How amazing—the light of the world compared to the Temple's brightest torchlight! Neutrality in response to *Yeshua's* claim was impossible!

Jesus kept building on scriptural foundations, awakening people to their true meanings, and proclaiming their fulfillment in Himself. The Gospel accounts of His passion week take place in relationship to the feast of the Passover. After He rose from the grave, it eventually became obvious to believers that Jesus' death and resurrection had actually fulfilled the Spring Feasts, and exactly on God's prophetic timetable!

FEAST MEANINGS CONTINUED
AFTER THE MESSIAH'S ASCENSION

Reported in Acts, soon after Jesus' ascension, God then pours out His Spirit on believers fifty days after Passover, at the Feasts of Weeks (later in Greek called "Pentecost," the Greek word for "fifty"). Scholars say that God's timing for pouring out the Spirit on that day (50 days after the yearly Passover) matched the giving of the Law to Moses on Mount Sinai (approximately 50 days after the Hebrew's original Passover). Note that a couple of decades later, Jewish followers of Jesus were still keeping the Feasts. Right after Passover, the Apostle Paul was "hurrying to get to Jerusalem by Pentecost" (Acts 20:16). Today's Jewish communities—whether rejecting or accepting Jesus as the Messiah—still relate to the Feasts. We will not appreciate the timing and atmosphere of their celebrations today without being awake to those cultural facts.

The New Testament community, while almost totally Jewish the first few decades, soon snowballed into Gentile areas like Syria and Macedonia. As recorded in Acts 15, the ruling Jewish believers' Jerusalem Council came to a history-shaping agreement over the difficult question of law-keeping. Peter appealed to what he had been seeing the Lord doing among Gentiles, saying, "God, who knows the heart, showed that he accepted them by giving them the Holy Spirit, just as he did to us" (Acts 15:8). The Council came to a determination: 'No! We believe it is through the grace of our Lord Jesus Christ that we are saved, just as they are" (Acts 15:11).

TWO BLESSINGS

Gentile believers in *Yeshua* were thereafter not required to keep the law, which included circumcision, and also the feasts of Israel. However, there is still much to be learned from spiritual principles revealed in the precepts of the Mosaic covenant. In his Gospel, John the Apostle gives honor to both Old and New Testament revelations, saying, "From the fullness of his grace we have all received one blessing after another. For the law was given through Moses; grace and truth came through Jesus Christ" (John 1:16-17).

THE PROPHETIC LEVEL

It is often pointed out that prophecies in Scripture frequently relate to a prophet's own situation, or to something in their near future, and/or to happenings in a far distant time of fulfillment. Like the old three-section spyglass that could be pulled out further, true prophecies might be fulfilled in the prophet's lifetime, or soon thereafter, or at a distant time, awaiting future fulfillment. For example, after the angel revealed much to Daniel—predicting mysterious scenarios in the future—he concluded by saying, "Go your way, Daniel, because the words are closed up and sealed until the time of the end" (Daniel 12:9). Daniel lived as a captive in Persia around 500 BC, and "the end" has not yet come. Similarly, the pattern of the feasts played a contemporary role in the Hebrew community's real time, but on their prophetic level, they also point to fulfillments yet to take place in the future.

OVERLOOKED?

The seven feasts are introduced in Leviticus, as well as Exodus, Numbers, and Deuteronomy. Throughout Old and New Testaments, feast celebrations repeatedly come into the text. The proclamation of the finale, the Jubilee, is given in Leviticus 25, although its practice does not appear often thereafter. Perhaps to Hebrew celebrants then, and also to people now, "once in a lifetime" could seem far enough in the future to ignore. From an eschatological viewpoint, however, blindness to God's ultimate goal would not make sense.

CLOSER, CLOSER, CLOSER

But leaving the feasts' prophetic level to explore later, let me return to when the Jubilee intersected our own life in a new way. The Jubilee concept that was first brought to our attention in Kenya has been a catalyst in our thinking about Old Testament relevance. But I'd given little thought to the specific Jubilee aspect of the feasts until our fiftieth wedding anniversary loomed ahead. By then, we had already missed applying Jubilee insights or principles to other fiftieth milestones—like fifty years of age, or fifty since graduation, or fifty years of parenthood, or of a career, etc. Picturing typical fiftieth wedding anniversary cake-and-punch parties, we preempted what might be devised by others and threw a surprise 45th anniversary celebration for our sons, their wives, and our grandchildren.

"ONE-EIGHTH"

Weddings harken back to family histories. Homes are built on foundations, from which rise one generation's story after another. Between us, Charlie and I had three grandparents whose nationalities were a mixture of English, German, and French. Only one was a "pure" anything—Charlie's mother, whose parents were both Swedish immigrants to America in the early 1900s. (Charlie liked to claim that he was one-half Swede, our sons one-fourth, grandchildren one-eighth.) His father had decided it would be fun to have the family celebrate Swedishness. That translated into serving *lutefisk* and pickled herring at a meal during Christmastime, and trips to holiday events in Kansas' "little Sweden," a small town named Lindsborg.

BORROWED CHRISTMASTIME SANCTUARY

On our 45th wedding anniversary, we took our nuclear family of sixteen to Lindsborg's Swedish Crown restaurant, delightful with its Scandinavian décor and traditional smorgasbord dinner, *lutefisk,* pickled herring and all. Each year, on the day after Christmas, the white steepled old church on main street held a Swedish language service at 2:00. The church would still be warm at 3:00, so we asked for permission to borrow their sanctuary with its festive greens, grand piano, and Christmas tree in the chancel, under which I placed thirteen little boxes of "heritage gifts." Each family member had a part in the service, and Charles and I got to testify to our sons and grandchildren how we had come to know Jesus in our college days, and tell about ways He had led and blessed us all through the years. Standing at the church door when leaving, we watched our younger generations playing soccer in the church yard. Lit by the gold of the sunset, our 45th glowed with happiness for the bride, the groom, and the whole family.

SO, THE 50TH?

Four years later, when our 50th was approaching, I began exploring Leviticus for new inspiration and challenges. I discovered that great guidelines could be gleaned from God's Fiftieth Year plan. Why not see whether marriage and family could find blessing in them? So, we began experimenting.

3 ONE HOUSE, TWO STORIES:
Old & New Testament unity.
Is that continuity appreciated?

✎ How much have you been aware of the Bible's unity throughout both Covenants?

✎ Read Jesus' announcement of the "reality" of His identity in Luke 4:14-22, claiming to fulfill the earlier "shadow" passage in Isaiah 61:1-3. What do you think your response would have been, if you'd been a Jewish person in the crowd, and you understood Jesus' meaning?

✎ Their lambs' blood saved Israelites from death, in Egypt. The Exodus Passover foreshadows the blood of the Lamb of God on Calvary, saving believers from death. How do these ties deepen your understanding of Jesus' institution of the Last Supper?

Chapter 4
WEDDING JUBILEE

Facing our 50th Anniversary, I should explain that the year we got married, as a result of Charlie's Med School schedule and my mother's illness, the only day we could manage a wedding was Sunday, December 26th. We soon discovered that almost nobody welcomed another celebration on December 26th, the day after Christmas finding most families in collapse. So, over the years, we developed a habit of not mentioning our big day, but sneaking off to a quiet room in some hotel, having breakfast in bed, opening Christmas cards we'd not had time to read, etc. However, you can't really hide out on your 50th because your growing-up-family are clued in. This configuration prompted me to think ahead about that fateful day, and Jubilee possibilities came to mind.

During our 49th year, Charlie and I were enjoying serendipitous getaways at a hidden pond where we were allowed to occasionally spend quiet hours in the beauty of nature—sharing sun, walks, sandwiches, coffee, reading... all quite restorative. Musing over how one's 50th tied to the Jubilee, I began pondering the elements of Leviticus 25, wondering how we could incorporate them into our marriage Jubilee year.

R ... R... R... R...

Aspects began to stand out. In an English translation of the Bible, I noticed that "R" words are scattered throughout the chapter: rest, return, redeem, release—all restoration words. Now admittedly, applying these "R's" to our own situation was taking them out of the passage's context. We are first to understand what Scriptures mean to the people to whom they were addressed at the time they were given. But we are also to learn from these examples, and apply their principles to our own lives.

THE ORIGINAL CONTEXT

When the Jubilee "R's" were instituted for Israel, the terms in Hebrew probably didn't start with the letter R. Nevertheless, that's what I had to work with. Looking up cross-references with Leviticus 25, I discovered that this Jubilee concept kept surfacing in Jewish history in ways a Gentile might not even notice. In the very chapter where Israel is told that they are to be a light to the Gentiles, the Spirit of God gives Isaiah a prophecy using Jubilee language: "The Redeemer, the Holy One of Israel says ... salvation ... covenant ... restore the land ... in the time of my favor ... reassign inheritances ... say to the captives, 'be free!'" (See Isaiah 49:7-9. Verses 8-9 are in full on p. 108.)

We noticed the significance, in chapter 3, of the fact that Jesus announced His identity in the synagogue in Nazareth by quoting Isaiah's prophetic wording—"the year of the Lord's favor"—and applying it to its arrival in Himself (pp. 39-40). (See Isaiah 61:1-2.) As we noted, His hearers could grasp the meaning of these code words Jesus used, and they tried to kill Him for it. (See Luke 4:14-30.) With little Old Testament background, today's reader could easily miss the depth of meaning that had come into play. Oh, how much Gentiles have to learn from the Hebrew Scriptures!

BACK TO MY ENGLISH "R'S"

But now is now, I reasoned, and the Scriptures are to be our "training in righteousness" (II Timothy 3:16). So, how could we apply those "R's" in our own lives? How might we "rest, or return, or release" in some sense? And how could we ourselves do any "redeeming," since we're warned that the work of redemption can only be accomplished by God? (See Ephesians 2:8.)

REST

Originally, the Jubilee pattern built in rest for the workers and even the land, leaving it fallow every seven years and the fiftieth. Rest is a hard requirement in our non-agrarian (but still workaholic) times. Retirement years do allow for rest, but I was not a "resting" person. How might I apply this principle? Strangely, illness provided my opportunity. Before Christmas of our 49th year, I fortuitously got the flu.

Woe is me, I thought, *with Christmas approaching and here lies grandmother in bed!* I lay there staring at my own grandmother's walnut dresser from Pennsylvania—still in the family. It was in my room when I was around the ages of my seven grandchildren. I returned in thought to my youth, remembering life between ages seven and thirteen at 311 North 7th Street in my Kansas home town. A connected thought bubbled up from a summer with my aunt and uncle in Missouri in my 14th year. When canoeing in the evenings on Lake Taneycomo, I'd tell

Uncle Bernie fun things my brother and I did in our childhood. "You ought to write a book when you grow up," Uncle Bernie used to chuckle, "and call it, 'I Remember Saturdays.'"

Now here I lay so many years later, remembering his suggestion. I began speculating, *What story from when I was seven would my seven-year-old-grandson Luke like? What story from my ninth year might nine-year-old Joanna enjoy? What would thirteen-year-old Ethan identify with?* I sat up and started writing. My Christmas gift that year turned out to be a booklet of stories called, "I Remember Saturdays." The first page of each chapter that was addressed to one of our seven grandchildren featured their own cameo-shaped photo. They loved having their own chapter in a book written just for them. The whole project took me back to my childhood home, returning to my beginnings.

RETURN

Actually, the "return" command nudged us to make some trips to our hometown roots and people. Some natural returns are built into one's sixties and seventies—re-gatherings for high school or college reunions, or for retirement parties, or even for memorial services. One's wedding anniversary harkens back to where it took place, often in the hometown. By the time a person is in this celebratory season, the folks and the homeplace may be deteriorating, and the boys and girls of childhood memories will have been scattered. But enfolded into God's Jubilee instructions, we can discern the sacredness of the gender, race, family, and country into which each person has been born. These unique endowments are not random; they are not to be taken lightly, but are to be honored as gifts.

RELEASE

Release was an aspect of the Jubilee's "Rs" that I had to puzzle over to find a personalized equivalent. Going to the biblical situation in Hebrew history, people were facing stark physical realities of indentured service and even slavery. If not already redeemed by someone having paid their redemption price, servants and slaves were to be released in the Jubilee Year. All land that had been sold in hard times was to be returned to the original family. All debts were to be forgiven, and impoverishment ended. What a radical reorganization of society! I thought back to the lecturers in Kenya. They had pointed out the various inabilities of capitalism, socialism, or communism to deal with our human perversities that lead to landlessness, generational poverty, oppression, serfdom, and slavery.

INTER-PERSONAL RELATIONSHIPS

Corporately, our American society also struggles with these aspects, but at this time, I was only trying to work on my own back yard. *Do I have similar blighted relationships?* I wondered. Many of us have people we've held captive too close, or else distanced ourselves from. Most of us have grudges to release, and relationships to mend. *In my relationships,* I pondered, *whom might I be holding captive in any form of emotional slavery, or by whom am I still being held in an unhealthy way? Is there a relationship to restore? A grudge to lay aside? Someone I should go to for forgiveness? Some uncomfortable unfinished "business," someone with something against me or me against her, or him?*

Mending those ruptures required honest self-searching, thoughtful prayer, and sometimes led to difficult communications, re-connections, or reparations. There is nothing better for repairing a broken relationship and restoring fellowship than admitting wrong and asking forgiveness.

DIVESTMENT

The application of the *release* principle also suggests a more physical possibility, the action that our sons call "divestment." Divestment of the stuff that has built up over years comes hard for elders, not that we would mind disposing of things. It's just that we can't face the decisions involved and the search for receivers. The fact is, really very little of our stuff would be all that meaningful or useful to anyone anyway. I began by giving my mother's Hammond organ to a new little church. I'd already released many family heirlooms by having given a boxed "heritage gift" to each in the family at our 45th Anniversary at the little white church, five years before.

A HAPPY DIVESTMENT EXPERIENCE

I pondered how we might turn divestment into family fun. Along our driveway stands a 12-foot by 20-foot storage shed where stuff from three generations languishes. (When my grandfathers each died, their widows broke up housekeeping and came to live with our family, hence the build-up.) Huge strides were made one bright summer day halfway through the Jubilee year when the whole extended family came home. "Heritage Day" we called it. After a family photograph and picnic, we spent the afternoon at a long table with benches in front of the "Stuff Shed." We gave each grandchild a packet of writing and drawing supplies for answering a Heritage Quiz and creating his or her own personal family crest. Meanwhile Charlie and I told family stories connected to the stuff we were unearthing out of the shed—a motley array of "treasures." Everybody had a card on which to write three things they'd most like. Each family kindly took home a big box. Charlie and I sighed happily to have found a few meaningful match-ups. After everybody left, we passed on some of the remainder to friends, libraries, antique shops, thrift stores, and, of course, our faithful weekly disposal service.

Passing our lives through the Jubilee grid helped us face the rest of our Golden Years together less troubled, less distracted, less weighed down with "unfinished business." In the 50th Anniversary year, we had the excuse and the motivation to execute "intentional divestments." Looking back, we realized that it was applying Jubilee elements all through the year that turned out to be our best gift to ourselves, and to our family as well.

REDEEM

Next to consider was the concept of "redemption." Redemption is at the heart of God's yearning for us to be restored to fellowship with Himself. The offer of redemption shines through passage after passage of God's Word to man. When Jesus on the cross cried out, "It is finished!"—it was the work of redemption that was completed.

Not surprisingly, Leviticus' foreshadowing of the ultimate Jubilee demonstrates its dependence on the finished work of the whole world's Redeemer. In Chapter 3, we looked at Scripture's double relationships, calling one "shadows" and the other "realities" (or "substance"). For instance, Hebrews 8:5 speaks of the earthly Tabernacle as "a copy and shadow of what is in heaven."

In the Jubilee's original "shadow" form, the fifty-year-processes included every generation's need for a "kinsman redeemer." The family's property was all to be restored to them at the Jubilee. In the interim, a kinsman redeemer could purchase it, and only he could perform this duty. The short book of Ruth gives us a glimpse of how the redeemer's role impacted family life in Israel. (Chapter 6 will explore the riches of that story.) Centuries later, Jesus was revealed to be the fulfillment of Ruth's "foreshadowing," when "reality" time arrived—when the Savior became the human family's Kinsman Redeemer for the whole world.

MY OWN REDEEMER

The New Covenant reveals that Jesus is God's ultimate Kinsman Redeemer for those who choose to be in His family. *Redemption* involves paying a price to take back something or someone that was lost or stolen. Each of us either accepts the Savior's sacrifice to redeem us from our lostness, or rejects His work on the cross to recover God's merciful intent for those He "so loves...that he gave his one and only Son," as John 3:16 words it.

There was nothing I could do to *apply* the "R" of His redeeming me except to rejoice in its having been done for me. It was coming to the Lord Jesus for redemption in my 20th year that birthed my whole re-orientation to life. A Jubilee increment later, the Spirit of God was still faithfully leading me in His ways, and informing my anticipation of His final Jubilee.

OUR FORMAL 50TH

Dear Reader, if you are wondering whether any celebration occurred on the actual day of our 50th anniversary, the answer is yes. But it happened in spite of our objection. We had pointed out the inevitable Christmas overload and that a third of the family were serving overseas. But our sons surprised us with a lovely luncheon with family and a few dear old friends on December 26, after all. As I've mentioned, we'd often just hidden out at a motel that day after Christmas. It had seemed to be a compassionate allowance for most people's "weariest day of the year." This one time though, after the luncheon, we took the whole family to an overnight at "The Barn," a rustic bed and breakfast with fun things to do and an indoor swimming pool. Fiftieth wedding anniversaries are not just for honoring a couple's marriage; they celebrate the ongoing blessing of the whole family constellation.

4 WEDDING JUBILEE: Our 50th Anniversary experiment. Note the "R's"!

✎ Where are you in relationship to your 50th year of life, high school graduation, marriage, parenthood, job, or some other milestone?

✎ From the 25th chapter of Leviticus, what "R" words do you notice?

✎ Which of the "R's" of the Jubilee stipulations suggests a personal application you'd find interesting to try?

Chapter 5

NO ATONEMENT, NO JUBILEE

I n my enthusiasm for finding principles that apply to the Fiftieth idea, I overlooked a very important aspect of the scriptural record. I was forgetting the clues, God's codes, especially regarding timing. Going to the texts which introduce the Jubilee, I faced up to a predecessor which I'd overlooked in Leviticus:

> "Say to the Israelites: 'On the <u>first day of the seventh month</u> you are to have a day of rest, a sacred assembly commemorated with <u>trumpet blasts</u>'" (Leviticus 23:24).

> "Count off seven sabbaths of years—seven times seven years—so that the seven sabbaths of years amount to a period of forty-nine years. Then have the trumpet sounded everywhere on the <u>tenth day of the seventh month; on the Day of Atonement</u> sound the trumpet throughout your land. Consecrate the fiftieth year and proclaim liberty throughout the land to all its inhabitants. It shall be a jubilee for you" (Leviticus 25:8-10).

The trumpet blasts on the day of the Feast of Trumpets were to warn the community about the coming Day of Atonement. The Day of Atonement had to precede the inauguration of the Jubilee Year. These timings and concepts are fascinating in their "foreshadowing" form, and they communicate "realities" that would eventually take place.

CODE CLUES

For instance, Trumpets came on the 1st day of the 7th month; then the Day of Atonement on the 10th of the 7th month. Digging into the Bible's mine of revelation, these clues take us down into a rich vein, the vein of the seventh month. (Incidentally, notice that on God's calendar all the feasts are scheduled in the first seven months, starting in about March/April. They are ordained to be celebrated in the growing season's months, the traveling months; warm months, not in the winter.) Trumpets announced occasions and warned the community. The fifth feast, called the Feast of Trumpets, proclaimed the soon-coming necessity to face judgment at the Day of Atonement, the sixth feast. The sixth was actually a day of fasting, of admission of sin, of repentance. Then five days later comes the week-long, seventh and final feast of the year, the Feast of Ingathering (or Booths). This series of annual feasts culminated each seventh year with "the Sabbath year," when even the land was to be given rest (Leviticus 25:1-7). Multiply the cluster of seven yearly feasts again by seven and arrive at the 49th year. Now the blood (code for death) of the atonement must deeply be applied. Cleansing and forgiveness must happen, before Jubilee celebration can take place the 50th year.

DAY OF ATONEMENT APPEARS THROUGHOUT SCRIPTURE

Once instituted in Leviticus, the Day of Atonement's presence in the Bible can be recognized by simply noting the two key dates: 1st and 10th of the seventh month. Leviticus 16:18-19 describes the day in detail with its sacrifices, its two goats (one for sacrifice and one the scapegoat), the blood of atonement, and the Great High Priest's role. Numbers 29:7-11 describes the Day's offerings. I Chronicles 6:49 states Aaron's role. In the New Testament, Hebrews 9:6-10 summarizes the Day of Atonement and identifies Jesus as the ultimate Great High Priest who made the atonement that fulfilled what that day foreshadowed.

TEN DAYS OF AWE

Why the 10-day interval between the Feast of Trumpets and the Day of Atonement? These days were provided for the Hebrews to humbly consider the approaching day of judgment before their awesome God. Such a certainty cried out for personal repentance, for relational reconciliations, and for repairing sin-based damages before facing the Judge of all the earth. This yearly ritual can remind the believing community even today of our need to humble ourselves before our Judge. We need to personally and corporately confess our sinfulness as we depend on the only source of atonement between God and man. (See I Timothy 2:5.)

PREFIGURED PROVISION

No sons or daughters of Adam can rely on taking the death penalty for our sins, for we couldn't survive. God had to take it upon Himself to provide the atonement. Very early in Hebrew history God acted out this enigma when He tested Abraham. The near tragedy on Mount Moriah ended with God providing the ram caught in the thicket to take the place of Abraham's son, Isaac. Abraham had trusted God to somehow intervene, for he had answered Isaac, "God himself will provide the lamb for the burnt offering, my son" (Genesis 22:8). That foreshadowed provision would be fulfilled centuries later, again on that same Mount Moriah. But no animal could be substituted when the heavenly Father's Son atoned for the world's sin.

DEEPER DOWN

Actually, the ongoing necessity for atonement was made clear from the very beginning when sin entered into the world. God had warned that disobeying His only command would bring forth sin, and sin would bring forth death (Genesis 2:17). Adam and Eve's catastrophic choice at the fall immediately issued in death—their own spiritual deaths and eventually their physical deaths. An animal's death would dramatize the reality as well, for the skin of an animal that was substituted for their own death penalty became their covering. From the fall onward, altars of sacrifice appear in the Patriarchal period. Sin always brings forth death in some way, and altars reminded people about sin's life-taking, blood-represented price. Notice that Noah's first act on dry ground was to build an altar (Genesis 8:20). Abraham built altars at Bethel (Genesis 12:8), and Hebron (Genesis 13:18), and most predictive of the final redemptive sacrifice, in type, he had to build the altar on which he nearly had to sacrifice Isaac (Genesis 22).

CRUCIAL DISCLAIMER: THE "R" THAT MUST PRECEDE ACCESS TO THE ULTIMATE JUBILEE

The principles in the Jubilee process can be creative and helpful to anyone. But without the cleansing from sin pictured in the Day of Atonement, the principles will not be as fully experienced or eternally settled in the lives of those who ignore the need for the Lord's provision of atonement. The "r" that must precede the others (return, redeem, release) is repentance! This limitation is a necessary disclaimer to face if one is trying to apply Jubilee principles. They really can only be fully experienced by those who acknowledge their need for the atonement God provided in His Son's sacrifice for their own sins.

WE LIVE WHEN "THE FULLNESS OF TIMES" IS CULMINATING

The Lord gave the Day of Atonement proclamation long before the foreshadowed atonement was provided by the sacrificial death of the Son. It pointed forward in shadow form to that actuality. "The law is only a shadow of the good things that are coming—not the realities themselves" (Hebrews 10:1).

We live after the cross and resurrection, the events that divide all history into BC and AD. Therefore, those living after the Incarnation can know how the preview enacted on the Day of Atonement was eventually fulfilled. The Day of Atonement reminds us that we cannot expect the full blessings of the Jubilee without having dealt with our personal need for the atonement that was mercifully accomplished by the Lamb of God.

We live today in the gap between the spring and fall feasts, the time Jesus in Luke 21:24 calls "the times of the Gentiles." The Apostle Paul reminds us that this period will eventually end, "when the full number of Gentiles come in" (Romans 11:25). That completion will lead to events that culminate in the final

Jubilee, to which all these "dress rehearsals" have pointed. We live at a time when almost the whole story has been recorded, and after both Testaments have been made available to us. Only the finale awaits fulfillment. The Scriptures make us aware of our own short gap between what can be our "practice Fifties" on earth and our participation in God's final Jubilee.

FORESHADOWS AND FULFILLMENTS

Let's be sure to understand why the foreshadowed Redeemer did appear in the world. A shadow can't exist without a reality throwing it across the landscape. All those early Old Testament shadows were cast from the reality of an execution tree up ahead in the world's time. Think of each drama that foresaw future fulfillment. The first Adam's introduction of sin into the world (Genesis 3) had to be dealt with by a seed of Adam (Romans 5:12-14). The interrupted sacrifice of Abraham's son Isaac (Genesis 22) had to reach fulfillment in the uninterrupted sacrifice of God's own Son (Romans 8:32). The Passover lamb's blood on the doorposts in Egypt (Exodus 12) had to be shed by the suffering Savior (Isaiah 53). The Great High Priest on the Day of Atonement had to sprinkle blood on the Ark in the Holy of Holies (Leviticus 16), but Jesus entered Heaven itself "once for all by his own blood, having obtained eternal redemption" (Hebrews 9:11-12). The Gospels report how the shadows were fulfilled by the Savior's cross and resurrection. These two realities continued to beam their truth and power forward into the rest of the New Testament. They still light the New Covenant family's lives throughout time.

THE REDEEMER'S PURPOSE

Jesus' primary Incarnational mission was not just to give us an example. He didn't come just to be a teacher, a healer, or even our dearest friend—although He serves God and humanity in these ways. Primarily He came to deal with humanity's sin problem. The main way the suffering servant of Isaiah 53 served was to <u>die.</u>

> But he was pierced for our transgressions, he was crushed for our iniquities; the punishment that brought us peace was upon him, and by his wounds we are healed. We all, like sheep, have gone astray, each of us has turned to his own way; and the LORD has laid on him the iniquity of us all (Isaiah 53:4-6).

In Gethsemane, what He was facing was so horrible that He asked the Father whether there could be some other way. But there was no other. "Now my heart is troubled, and what shall I say? 'Father save me from this hour?' No, it is for this very reason that I came to this hour" (John 12:27). Agonizing on the verge of the cross, He recoiled from what He and the Father had determined He was going to have to do. And why did He have to do it? Because no other sinless substitute was available. Because we sinners could not pay the price of our own sins. It is only because of His resurrection that believers can count on their own resurrection, only because of the Redeemer's work on the cross and His rising from death. "Because I live, you also shall live," He assured His disciples (John 14:19). His resurrection now sheds the light of His marvelous promise into the futures of those who trust the Savior.

THE NEW COVENANT FEAST

Jesus left His community no elaborate ceremonies and no provision for a codified pattern of apostolic secession. He promised that His Spirit would be His replacement, and instituted only one New Covenant feast, what we call "the Lord's Supper."

> When the hour came, Jesus and his apostles reclined at the table. And he said to them, "I have eagerly desired to eat this Passover with you before I suffer. For I tell you, I will not eat it again until it finds fulfillment in the kingdom of God." After taking the cup, he gave thanks and said, "Take this and divide it among you. For I tell you I will not drink again of the fruit of the vine until the kingdom of God comes." And he took bread, gave thanks and broke it, and gave it to them, saying, "This is my body given for you; do this in remembrance of me." In the same way, after the supper he took the cup, saying, "This cup is the new covenant in my blood, which is poured out for you" (Luke 22:14-20).

The early church began to celebrate the Lord's feast in terms of the past, present, and future. "Whenever you eat this bread and drink this cup, you proclaim the Lord's death until he comes" (I Corinthians 11:26). The New Covenant feast is panoramic. It stretches from the reality the Redeemer fulfilled in our past, to the reality which He will complete in our future, at His return.

Therefore, for us to fully appropriate these realities, we need to be sure our own lives match God's revealed timing. Receiving Christ's atonement must precede our entrance into the Jubilee that our Savior procured!

MY OWN APPROPRIATION

Dear Reader, I must admit that as a church-goer from childhood, those "communion Sundays" and "Easter Week services" came through to me as memorials to a man who died 2,000 years ago, a man who remains our example, the church's model for good living. I took communion, went to Easter week services, and tried to be as spiritual as I could muster. I learned to play the church organ, led the youth group, and considered myself to be a very nice girl. I led the marching band at school all four years, was a top student, etc. Then, the Friday night of our high school graduation weekend, our senior class held a skating party at nearby Sycamore Springs. A fellow graduate and I were called off the rink suddenly, and told we needed to go back to town. There had been an accident. Our fathers had left in a small chartered plane that morning for a meeting in Denver. In town we learned that in a storm, the plane had gone down, burned, and all five men had been killed.

Dr. Conrad had been our town's doctor and highly active promoter, his daughter's hero, my pride and my security. Grief struck our community, for everyone knew some of the five men. I was excused from a valedictorian speech at Baccalaureate. I can't remember Monday's graduation, and barely my father's funeral, amid the other four men's services. All summer, I would park Dad's car beside his grave at the cemetery, grieving his end, and trying to come to grips with death.

As a freshman at KU in the fall, I tried to emulate my father's attitude. He had stomped out of our church when I was a toddler, calling them "a bunch of hypocrites." I decided I should let religion go. Yet, I thought I should at least read the

New Testament through once, to be intellectually honest. I did so, but the Scriptures meant nothing to me. However, for community, I did hang out on Sunday nights at KU's Westminster Fellowship House. One night in January, two American women shared their experience in Germany after World War II. They had gone to help rebuild in the ruins. To thank them as they left the country, a little peasant woman gave them the one thing she had, her Bible. Somehow the story awakened self-examination.

On my way back to my Scholarship Hall, I wandered distraught into KU's little Danforth Chapel, kept open perpetually. All alone at the altar, I poured out probably my first recognition that I was a self-centered, arrogant wretch needing help beyond myself. Having heard little scriptural truth in our spiritually cold church back home, I had no idea how to get help, or that what was happening to me was, biblically speaking, "coming under conviction of sin." Not knowing what to do with my awakening, I simply wept out my desperation to God, praying, "Whatever you do for someone like me, God, please, please do it!" Right there and then, I became overwhelmed with a deep sense of His forgiveness.

Back at my dorm, girls I met in the hall looked surprised and asked, "What's happened to you?" Not knowing how to answer, I went out on the fire escape for the next hour and just kept saying, over and over, "Thank you, thank you, God!"

It would be seven months later before I learned "what God does for someone like me." A missionary physician pushed out of Korea by the war took over the medical practice my father left behind. Dr. Lowe recognized my spiritual neediness and offered to send me to a college leadership camp in the Rockies that he said was designed "to equip college students to reach high schoolers."

This most important week of my life took place in August before my sophomore year at KU. Jim Rayburn, Young Life's founder, had just obtained Frontier Ranch on Mt. Princeton. When Jim's poignant love for the Savior came through in his nightly teaching, the realness nearly broke my heart. During the days, I kept asking work crew guys and gals, "What makes you different?" In one way or another, their answers boiled down to, "I'm getting to know Jesus." Jim's secretary took me into the opening chapter of the Gospel of John. From the first eighteen verses, I learned Who Jesus actually was, and that He had been alive ever since the Resurrection, and always before that, and that I could know Him. When I discovered His identity, it made perfect sense to give myself unreservedly to Him.

"Now you've met, but you need to really get acquainted," they said. I asked how, and they said, "Take a Bible out under the pine trees tomorrow morning, and let Him talk to you, and you to Him." That started me on the path of intentionally meeting with Him most every day of my life. Suddenly the New Testament I'd found so meaningless just a year before came alive to me. I wondered why. As my spiritual understanding matured, I learned that when Jesus is received, His Spirit enters the believer's life. The Spirit of truth opens our eyes to what we are reading. His presence guides our hearts into deepening relationship with the Father who sent the Son into the world. Then they sent the Spirit in the Son's place, to actually indwell every believer who receives Jesus.

BE ASSURED

I share this, dear Reader, just to let you know how I discovered that I had to appropriate my dear Redeemer's atonement before my joy could begin. His offer of salvation wasn't based on going to church, trying to be good, or considering myself "a spiritual person." I needed to admit my need of forgiveness before God's holiness, and receive His provision for my reconciliation with Him through what His Son had done. He had taken my sin debt upon Himself. Therefore, my own experience undergirds my confidence in the biblical soundness of the title of this chapter, "no atonement, no jubilee." Our merciful God has been communicating that necessity throughout the Scriptures in one way after another, among them His truths in Israel's feasts. Yes, the Day of Atonement must surely precede our Jubilee.

5 NO ATONEMENT, NO JUBILEE:
Atonement to precede
the 50th year, and must precede
the ultimate Jubilee

✎ Leviticus 25:8-10, requires the necessity for atonement. Leviticus 16 lays out the Day's fuller procedures. How does Hebrews 9:23-28 help you apply those shadows to the reality of Jesus as our Great High Priest?

✎ In Abraham and Isaac's story in Genesis 22, what elements do you see in its "shadow" cast back from the "reality" of atonement that would later take place at that same location, on Mt. Moriah?

✎ When might you have asked God to apply the Son's atonement for your own sins to your need for forgiveness before Him? What brought you to that decision?

Chapter 6

CAMEO: A FAMILY STORY

The longest running dramatic serial in radio history (1932-1959) was called "One Man's Family." A generation later, "The Waltons" on TV drew people into another man's family life. The Waltons ran from 1971-1981, depicting the life and trials of a 1930s-1940s Virginia mountain family through the Great Depression and World War II. Somehow these windows into personal lives speak to our own; mirroring our own struggles, sorrows, and joys. And they highlight the irreplaceable value and role of each individual within a family.

Family is God's idea. God ordains "home" to be sacred. A godly home can act like earth's temporary substitute for the warmth of Heaven. The Jubilee stipulations were designed to protect each family, and their homeplace. Whatever losses, sorrows, and sins had overcome a family over the fifty years, they might be redeemed and restored in the Jubilee year.

A JUBILEE GEM

The little four-chapter book of Ruth gives us a window into one episode in the saga of the Messianic family. During a famine in Israel in the period of the Judges, the family of Elimelech from Bethlehem migrates to Moab. Their two sons marry Moabite women, but both husbands die, as does their father, leaving Naomi and her two daughters-in-law widowed.

Ruth pledges herself to Naomi, vowing that "your people shall be my people, and your God my God." Returning to Bethlehem with Ruth after the famine, Naomi yearns for continuation of the family line.

According to the Jubilee stipulations, the continuation of the family's land ownership was dependent upon a family's son, a "kinsman redeemer." As a widow, Naomi was unable to produce such an heir.

For Naomi's husband's land to be kept in the family, it had to be purchased by a kinsman redeemer. According to Leviticus 25:25-28, in the fiftieth year, everyone automatically got their land back. However, in non-Jubilee years, a kinsman redeemer could redeem it.

In Naomi's story, a noble landowner named Boaz admires and desires Ruth. By marrying Ruth, according to Jubilee procedures, Boaz becomes deceased Elimelech's family's kinsman redeemer. Out of Ruth and Boaz's union, their son Obed is born. Obed becomes the family's next kinsman redeemer. Eventually Obed has a son named Jesse, and Jesse fathers a son named David. Moabite Ruth thus became great-grandmother of Israel's King David!

This little family story—recorded centuries before its profound outworking—demonstrates the Jubilee's role through which God brings about His purposes. When Obed was born, "The women said to Naomi, 'Praise be to the LORD, who this day has not left you without a kinsman redeemer. May he become famous throughout Israel!'" (Ruth 4:14) Yes, superbly famous! Baby Obed eventually becomes grandfather of King David— who foreshadows God's Messianic King. Centuries later, to this family line which has carefully been kept intact, in Bethlehem of Judea Jesus is born, the Messiah, the whole world's Kinsman Redeemer!

GRACE FOR THE GENTILE

Scripture does not fail to point out God's love for those outside of His covenant community. He frequently reminds Israel that they, too, were once aliens in Egypt. He provides for the poor and the alien by commanding that they be allowed to glean grain in the Israelite fields, as did alien Ruth. (See Ruth 2:2, related to Leviticus 23:22.) Scripture makes a point to record especially the alien women who married into the family line of the Messiah. The first chapter of Matthew records Jesus' genealogy by the family line's fathers. However, two alien women are pointed out: "...Salmon the father of Boaz, whose mother was *Rahab*, Boaz the father of Obed, whose mother was *Ruth*, Obed the father of Jesse, and Jesse the father of King David" (Matthew 1:5-6). God's purpose and grace include aliens too! Jews naturally identify with this story, but alien Gentiles can see themselves in it as well, if they, like Rahab and Ruth, commit themselves to Israel's God.

UNIVERSAL LONGINGS

Applications to our own lives rise out of this story. People universally experience famines in life, not only food famines, but justice famines, companionship famines, famines for love. We get cut back, lose all manner of things—our dreams, our innocence, our loved ones, our inheritance, our peace. Ruth's commitment calls us to Naomi's God. Reflected in her story, we recognize our own longing for restoration. We long for rest and joy in the Home only the ultimate Kinsman Redeemer can provide.

THE MYSTERY OF THE SANDAL

The text of Ruth's story explains a curious cultural practice. The NIV puts Ruth 4:7 in parenthesis: "(Now in earlier times in Israel, for the redemption and transfer of property to become final, one party took off his sandal and gave it to the other. This was the method of legalizing transactions in Israel.)" The candidate who couldn't buy Elimelech's property had to remove his sandal in front of witnesses and give it to Boaz to give testimony to their transaction. Similarly, we find ourselves unprepared to pay for our own redemption. Mirroring that legal aspect of our redemption, each of us needs to "do business with the Lord." We have to admit our inability to redeem ourselves, and decide to "give our sandal" to the only Kinsman Redeemer who can save us from losing all the inheritance and joys of the Jubilee. Mercifully, no one need wait for the fiftieth year to "do business with Jesus." He can redeem us any time, and thus become, so to speak, our Jubilee!

RUTH/ROMANIA/NARNIA CONNECTIONS

Each culture has its own jurisdictions over how the wider community impacts personal lives. Naomi and Ruth's were imprinted with God's laws. History records each nation's methods. Story tellers can even create metaphorical societal scenarios. C. S. Lewis did that in his Narnia Series. (I read those seven books to our sons, John, Tim, and Nat, when they were grade school age in Ethiopia. Adventuring in Narnia was a great way to enjoy our time together during my six weeks in bed with hepatitis!) C. S. Lewis created amazing metaphors set in a variety of ages, jurisdictions, populations, and other worlds—in natural and unnatural environments. His characters correspond both seriously and playfully to reality and super-reality, to people we have known, and sentiments we ourselves have felt.

Curiously enough, C. S. Lewis' depiction of a ruined world cursed by the White Witch now reminds me of a ruined city Charles and I found ourselves in decades later, amid a European country's people ground down by lives of poverty and fear. Romanians had spent four decades in sort of a full-nation communist concentration camp. In the summer of 1990, Dr. Charlie was asked to be the medical officer going in with a group of German and Austrian young people to Galatz, Romania, on the Black Sea. Their organizers had been clandestinely helping underground believers in Romania during Nicolae Ceausescu's communist dictatorship, which lasted 42 years. With his iconic execution on Christmas day of 1989, the door opened for outsiders to go in to help. Among the horrors uncovered from those years of oppression and austerity were scores of emaciated AIDs-infected infants warehoused in their beds, and orphanages full of deserted or disabled children being held in pitiful conditions. Our Agape group took in a huge truck loaded with plumbing equipment, in order to repair nearly defunct bathrooms and showers in Galatz' orphanages, and to simply give loving attention to the children.

On our way out of Romania via the capital, I cringed seeing Ceausescu's mammoth, sprawling palace in Bucharest. The day before flying out, we crawled up six flights of stairs to spend the night with Romanian friends who lived in one of the city's monolithic, stark gray cement high rises. The whole scene reminded me of C. S. Lewis' underworld city turned into ruins by the Witch – Aslan's enemy. Battered subjects kept under her spell labored in darkness, fear, and servitude. To an outsider arriving in Romania out of the free world, evidence of the tyrant's curse seemed to have permeated Romanian culture with endemic despair, distrust, apathy, and for many, an escape into drunkenness. With the overthrow of Ceausescu, Romanians were suddenly allowed freedom within, and contacts from abroad. I think they may have found the presence of alien visitors to be so unnatural as to cause a mixture of uneasiness, relief, and yet joy. While among underground believers who had suffered so, we were greatly blessed by their spiritual depth learned in the fellowship of His sufferings.

The Romanian experience speaks to me of the weightiness of a ruler's tremendous responsibility. It leads me to compare God's patterns for authority and restoration with the unbelieving world's brutal methods of societal recalibration under totalitarian rule. History demonstrates the horrors of civilization after civilization that suffered ruination under heartless rulers. People talk of globalism today, as if it would be a utopia. But if humanity would ever submit to a world-wide ruler, fear would inevitably be the enforcing mechanism. Such a ruler is predicted in Revelation 13. The world's pattern is dependent on power; only God's rule is founded on love. The coming reign of the Messianic King is humanity's only sure hope for an actual Kingdom of righteousness and peace. Jesus promised, "But seek first his kingdom and his righteousness, and all these things will be given to you as well" (Matthew 6:33).

UNIVERSAL TEMPTATION: IDOL WORSHIP

Ruth and Boaz' story wasn't fiction; it actually happened. The book of Ruth is a little window into a past age, when God's covenant people were in fresh relationship with Him, and He was giving them guidelines. Today, after the Lord's sacrifice for the sins of the world has been made, the Messianic family has widened out to include Gentiles who embrace Him. Yet from antiquity until now, humanity has largely gone after idols, just like the Hebrews frequently did, and as today's cultures still do. Dedication to modern idols may seem more sophisticated than worshipping wood and stone, but idolizing various substitutes still demonstrates the same unfaithfulness to our Creator. The Bible tells us that the accounts of our forebears' responses to God are to serve a stated purpose:

> These things happened to them as examples and were written down as warnings for us, on whom the fulfillment of the ages has come (I Corinthians 10:11).

Numbers 25:1-3a records one episode of Israel's seduction:

> While Israel was staying in Shittim, the men began to indulge in sexual immorality with Moabite women, who invited them to the sacrifices to their gods. The people ate and bowed down before these gods. So Israel joined in worshipping the Baal of Peor. ...

But God had warned His people:

> Keep all my decrees and laws and follow them, so that the land where I am bringing you to live may not vomit you out. You must not live according to the customs of the nations I am going to drive out before you. Because they did all these things, I abhorred them (Leviticus 20:22-24).

WORLD-WIDE ACCESS!

Israel was to keep clear of the sin of idolatry with its false gods, child-sacrifice, and sexual perversions. Nevertheless, God was not unconcerned about the rest of the Gentile world lost in their own sins. He provided salvation for all. When the Savior died for the sins of humanity in Jerusalem, the curtain that kept all but the Great High Priest out of the Holy of Holies split open to the world (Luke 23:45). And when the risen Jesus, the ultimate Great High Priest, entered heaven's Holy of Holies and was exalted, the Spirit was suddenly poured out upon believers in Jerusalem (See Acts 2:33). Exactly on the schedule of God's feast calendar, as noted earlier, this happened the morning of the Feast of Weeks, which we now call "Pentecost."

The miracle of God's Good News uttered in multiple languages let the marvelous message escape the limitations of Hebrew and Aramaic to be heard in languages spoken throughout the world. New Testament teaching thereafter recognized Jews and Gentiles (the non-Jewish rest of the world) on an equal basis, since the Messianic progression and redemptive purpose had been accomplished:

> For he himself is our peace, who has made the two one and has destroyed the barrier, the dividing wall of hostility, by abolishing in his flesh the law with its commandments and regulations. His purpose was to create in himself one new man out of the two, thus making peace, and in this one body to reconcile both of them to God through the cross, by which he put to death their hostility (Ephesians 2:14-18).

Jew and Gentile could be united. Of course, this unification might set in motion relationships leading to marriage. Believers' marriages are not regulated by ethnicity or race, but only by faithful oneness in the Lord (II Corinthians 6:14-16).

GOD'S DEEPLY SIGNIFICANT ULTIMATE METAPHOR

The faithfulness of a believing husband and wife serves as a biblical metaphor of the Son's relationship to His bride, the corporate body of Christ. This precious representation is the reason biblically-motivated Christians find assaults upon God's ordination of marriage to be so painful. Smashing the beauty and holiness of sex and marriage as God ordained them not only destroys family life but also blinds people from "seeing" God's love through family life. In God's revealed Word, it is the metaphor of marriage—the love of the Bridegroom and Bride—with which the Bible comes to its climax (Revelation 19:7; 21:9; 22:17). God's deeply significant metaphor of marital union bestows on humanity a profound key to the meaning of life.

Our Kinsman Redeemer has paid the price of our redemption, but He waits for our answer to His passionate proposal, "Will you be my bride?"

6 CAMEO, A FAMILY STORY: The book of Ruth's drama about the Kinsman Redeemer

✎ Reading through the book of Ruth, what do you find to be a key to its message? Notice one concept which especially appears in these verses in Ruth: 2:20; 3:2, 9, 12; and 4:1, 3, 6, 8, 14.

✎ What idolatries do you see in our culture today? Are any particularly difficult for you?

✎ What are your convictions about the sanctity of gender, sex, marriage, family, and their relationship to God's message to humanity?

Chapter 7
COVENANT COROLLARY

W e are turning now to a key aspect of the Jubilee— the connection to God's covenant with Israel, sometimes called His *wife.* Today, the covenant-like bond we are most familiar with is the marriage covenant, called "marriage vows." My dear Charlie took our vows very seriously, a commitment that deeply secured our marital relationship. The family probably remembers Dad insisting that we repeat our vows before them at wedding anniversaries, like the 45th in Lindsborg, the 50th in Topeka, and the 60th, when we gathered together on Kitten Creek Road nine months before Charlie's graduation to Home.

NO PRACTICE, BUT FAITHFUL

Dr. Lowe's hurry-up advice (due to what he thought was Mother's near departure) got us married in just a month. On the night of our wedding rehearsal, the groom got distracted by a woeful hitchhiker's predicament on a cold Christmas night as Charlie was driving the hundred miles to my home. He took the poor man to his destination, but missed our wedding practice! One thing he never deviated from, however, was our vows. We were new believers who were taking God's Word seriously, and committing key verses to memory. Marriage vows taken before God—"in the name of the Father, the Son, and the Holy Spirit"—

seemed to be on the level of needing total internalization. So, my dear husband-to-be insisted that we memorize them, rather than repeating them at the prompting of the pastor. And in his mind, the promises being made were not just for the service; they were lifelong vows to keep in the forefront of our minds and hearts. Therefore, on wedding anniversaries he would always have us vow them again to each other privately, and when possible, before our family publicly, as well. Unknown to others, also saying our vows to each other became our custom before entering into physical marital union. What a lovely way to affirm the holiness of marriage, and to give thanks to the One who created this tremendously joyous gift of consummation to husbands and wives, and to us in particular!

JUBILEE-CONNECTED COVENANT

Vows can be entered into shakily, not realizing the cost of breaking them. The principles of Leviticus 25 minus the accountability of chapter 26 would rob the reader of incentives to "keep covenant" with the God of Israel, and thus be wonderfully blessed. Missing chapter 26 would leave the reader unprepared for what God said to expect if His covenant people did not share His heart, were not willing to walk in His ways, were unwilling to obey their LORD. His warnings are sobering. The 26th chapter of Leviticus sounds very similar to Moses' predictions in Deuteronomy 28. Both passages encourage God's beloved to be obedient in order to be blessed, and warn her not to disobey and incur judgment for breaking covenant with her LORD.

DISOBEDIENCE ON DISPLAY

The Old Testament faithfully records Israel's ongoing history of sin, repentance, restoration, then sliding back into idolatry over and over. The five books of the Torah lay out God's covenant instructions, and then the rest of the Old Testament gives us the history of Israel's response to the LORD their God. The Bible frankly admits what happened when Israel lost their love for Him, recorded in Joshua, Judges, and the books of Samuel, Kings, and Chronicles. Woven into this long history are the books of the prophets who spoke for God to Israel during these times. True prophets warned and wooed God's "beloved," but were persecuted for doing so. Scripture doesn't hide the unfaithfulness that crept in, and what it cost the "wife" God had chosen. The judgments prophesied did happen, just as God's true prophets had warned.

JESUS' HEART LOVE AND HEART BREAK

During God's incarnational appearance on earth, Jesus revealed the Good News of God's passionate desire to be received by His beloved. He offered totally unmerited forgiveness to anyone who would truly "hear" Him. On the other hand, Jesus also called Israel to account for rejecting their Messiah—Himself.

> Weeping, the Savior cried out, Oh Jerusalem, Jerusalem, you who kill the prophets and stone those sent to you, how often I have longed to gather your children together, as a hen gathers her chicks under her wings, but you were not willing. Look, your house is left unto you desolate. For I tell you, you will not see me again until you say, "Blessed is he who comes in the name of the Lord" (Matthew 23:37-39).

We cannot overlook wave after wave of Jesus' warnings and woes as He approached His mis-named "triumphal entry" into Jerusalem on the 10th of the first month, and His sacrifice as the Lamb of God on the 14th. (Notice God's exact biblical code dates—pointed out in Chapter 2.) Jesus' warnings are recorded in many chapters: Matthew 21-25, Mark 13, and Luke 21. They dare not be omitted from "the end of the story."

COVENANT-BREAKING WARNINGS

Going back to Leviticus' incentives and warnings, eight times in the 26th chapter God refers to the *covenant*—the covenant made between God and His people Israel. He keeps begging them not to break their side of the covenant, and assures them He does not break His. If they would keep the covenant, observing His sabbaths and obeying His decrees, then He promised that they would be rewarded with agricultural plenty, national safety, and generational fruitfulness. If they violated the covenant and rejected His decrees, they could expect decline, fruitlessness, famine, and oppression. He would rebuke them for their pride and rebellion repeatedly, yet offer them forgiveness, hoping for their repentance. But if they remained hostile, they could expect to be nearly destroyed, be defeated by enemies, scattered, and their land laid waste.

This 26th chapter of warnings ends with the prediction that Israel would be scattered—which turns out to be their Babylonian captivity. "For the land will be deserted by them and will enjoy its sabbaths while it lies desolate without them. They will pay for their sins because they rejected my laws and abhorred my decrees" (Leviticus 26:43). When the Chronicles of Israel were recorded, this result was confirmed again. (Notice that the Hebrew translation of the Old Testament places Chronicles, not Malachi, at the end.) II Chronicles' last chapter of the Hebrew Scriptures, speaking of Nebuchadnezzar, states the case:

> He carried into exile to Babylon the remnant who escaped from the sword, and they became servants to him and his sons until the kingdom of Persia came to power. The land enjoyed its sabbath rests; all the time of its devastation it rested, until the seventy years were completed in the fulfillment of the word of the LORD spoken by Jeremiah (II Chronicles 36:20-21).

All those 490 years of disobeying the seventh year sabbath of the land had to be accounted for. The LORD God is precise with His promises, His warnings, His predictions, His discipline, and with His calendar!

WHAT ABOUT US?

Just as we've considered how to apply God's life principles for Israel to our own personal lives, we should not avoid facing the Jubilee's warnings to those who choose to be disobedient to their Maker. God keeps His word, even if it means judgment. On the other hand, those who respond in faith to our Lord's loving purposes can be assured of unparalleled jubilation when He comes to us, or we return to Him in our Father's home.

COVENANT: A MASTER KEY

The Bible's on-going repetition of the word *covenant* signals the crucial role of covenant in the story of God's relationship with His people. Theologians speak of "the Abrahamic covenant" and "the Mosaic covenant." How those two were entered into can be found in passages like Genesis 15 and 17, and

Exodus 19 and 24. We need to understand that God's relationship to His people was sealed in a covenantal manner, like
a wedding. As the painful life and poignant message of the
prophet Hosea demonstrated, Israel was in covenantal relationship to God, like a wife to her husband. Her unfaithfulness was
adulterous. Giving herself to an idol broke her covenant, and
broke her husband's heart.

In Leviticus 26, six times the statement is made: "I am the
LORD." Remember who you are married to! The first of His
Ten Commandments echoes down through history: "I am the
LORD your God, who brought you out of Egypt, out of the land
of slavery. You shall have no other gods before me" (Exodus
20:1-3). Those reminders are as if He is calling her to remember
their vows, and to stay faithful to the One who is her covenantal
partner.

FAST FORWARD TO NOW

The biblical record is not only history. It is a priceless
gift that is meant to be assimilated and applied so that any
generation of God's people may be blessed, as well. We don't
only read the Bible; the Bible reads us. It asks us, too, "Are
you being faithful to the God who made you, brought you out
of your own slaveries—the One who enfolded you into His
covenantal love?"

A CHANGE IN RELATIONSHIP TO MOSAIC LAWS

This is a good time to clarify a natural question, wondering
if our relationship to Old Testament laws now is different—
after the Incarnation. Yes, it is mercifully different. The Savior's

blood ratifies a New Covenant with Israel that Gentiles now may be adopted into. As Jeremiah prophesied,

> "The time is coming," declares the LORD, "when I will make a new covenant with the house of Israel and with the house of Judah. It will not be like the covenant I made with their forefathers when I took them by the hand to lead them out of Egypt, because they broke my covenant, though I was a husband to them," declares the LORD. "This is the covenant I will make with the house of Israel after that time," declares the LORD. "I will put my law in their minds, and write it on their hearts. I will be their God and they will be my people" (Jeremiah 31:31-33).

The life-less keeping of the Old Covenant's external rules was eventually to be replaced by the New Covenant's dynamic of heartfelt oneness!

A WINDOW ON THIS NEW COVENANT "HEART" REALITY

Dear Reader, may I digress briefly to share one of my own brushes with this new dynamic? In the first chapter, I described our surprise at finding Ethiopia to be the "African Zion." Those manifestations were connected to the north's ancient history, the Ethiopian Orthodox church, the Black Jewish community, and all their ties to Israel. On the other hand, after language school in the north, Dr. Bascom was stationed at Soddu Hospital in the south. There we met a whole different Ethiopia, a huge swath of the country that had languished in animism for centuries.

We found ourselves among first- and second-generation Christians in their first love for the Savior. Their community had encountered the Gospel in just the last four decades.

They knew no overlay of 20 centuries of Christendom's history. Instead, they were suddenly emerging out of spiritual darkness, their long ages of suffering under the rule of *Saitan*, into the light of God's love. Their joy was contagious.

We went wide-eyed to our first church service. The large haystack-shaped meeting place was constructed much like their homes, neatly thatched with grass right down to the ground. One door, no windows. When seated inside on three-legged stools at the periphery, we were the only foreigners among a hundred or more adults and children sitting on logs or mats on freshly cut grass. A skeletal ring of upright beams circled the room, bending down from a tall center pole to the structure's periphery.

As I looked up at that huge tree-trunk raised above us, I couldn't help thinking of Calvary. Music was a whole new experience with an unfamiliar five-tone scale, not our eight-tone sounds. Their indigenous songs were sung antiphonally, the leader singing a statement or question alternated with a congregational response. "Are you suffering?" the soloist would ask. "He suffered too!" the congregation would sing back. "Are you rejected?" ... "He was rejected too." "What is His promise?" ... "He will come again!" With no grapes in the area, local honey water and dark brown bread were their communion elements. For three hours, we listened to Scriptural messages in a tribal language completely foreign to us—confessions of sin, requests for intercession, professions of belief, punctuated by earnest prayers uttered prostrate with foreheads on the ground.

The whole experience couldn't have been farther from my youth's stained-glass and polished-wood sanctuary with organ, and robed choir marching in to "Holy, Holy, Holy." Sermons short on Scripture in my home church had never spoken deeply to me. I knew not a word of this former slave tribe's language and I was worshipping among a people of totally different race, history, and education than my own. Yet a benediction of heart oneness swept over me. And not only in services, but in daily life as we lived among these on-fire believers, I sensed a depth of faith, earnestness, and reality beyond my own. Truly, Pentecost's gathering in of peoples "unto the ends of the earth" in oneness around my Lord, their Lord, rose up before me.

THE COST OF GOD'S COVENANTS

Well, back to covenants. Their bloodiness fits better in the wilds of Ethiopia than in our sterile modern meat markets. Genesis 15 allows us to glimpse what "cutting a covenant" involved. An animal was slain, its two parts laid on the ground, with a bloody path between. The covenant partners walked through to affirm the seriousness of their commitment, as if to say, "May it be so done to me if I do not keep my oath." God put Abraham to sleep and the LORD went through the blood alone, significantly, knowing that Abraham, a son of Adam, would not have the strength to keep covenant. Blood (symbol of one's life) shed (symbol for death) was the covenantal key. At the Last Supper, centuries after the inauguration of Israel's covenant at Mount Sinai, Jesus took a cup and said, "This is my blood of the covenant, which is poured out for many for the forgiveness of sins" (Matthew 26:28). The next day, Passover day, the final Lamb of God would pour out His blood for the remission of sins, activating the New Covenant.

THE ENDURANCE OF HIS COVENANTS

Did Jesus revoke the first covenant? No! Jesus flatly stated: "Do not think that I have come to abolish the Law or the Prophets; I have come not to abolish them, but to fulfill them." (Matthew 5:17) He explained the two covenants in colloquial terms. "Neither do men pour new wine into old wineskins. If they do, the skins will burst, the wine will run out and the wineskins will be ruined. No, they pour new wine into new wineskins, and both are preserved." (Matthew 9:17)

The New Testament affirms both covenants and explains their relationship. Paul made this clear to the Galatians, explaining the role of the covenantal promise given to Abraham and the role of the law given to Moses.

> The promises were spoken to Abraham and to his seed. The Scripture does not say "and to seeds" meaning many people, but "and to your seed," meaning one person, who is Christ. What I mean is this: The law, introduced 430 years later, does not set aside the covenant previously established by God and thus do away with the promise (Galatians 3:16-17).

This passage further clarifies that righteousness could not come by the law, and then summarizes: "Now that faith has come, we are no longer under the supervision of the law." Faith in what? Not in the law, but in the promise. Faith in the One promised to Eve, then to Abraham, the "seed" who would eventually bless the world. It is faith in that "seed" that secures our righteousness in God's sight—Jesus' righteousness credited to us, not our own. That's grace!

"NEW WINE" WHEN?

When would this changeover take place? Here's where we will be helped by God's time codes discovered in the prophetic level of the Feasts. At His ascension, Jesus told his disciples to wait in Jerusalem. For what? When? Ten days later, fifty days after their Lord's crucifixion, they could not help fearing for their lives when crowds were converging again on Jerusalem for the Feast of *Shavuot*, the Feast of Weeks—meaning seven weeks after Passover. This one-day Feast, we learned earlier, memorialized the giving of the Law on Mount Sinai.

On that day we now call Pentecost (Greek for 50), the local believers and pilgrims from abroad who had journeyed to Jerusalem were shocked the morning of that Feast, as reported in Acts 2. Whatever was this miraculous pouring out of God's message in all their languages?! Previously a coward, Peter, suddenly filled with the Spirit, boldly announced: "God has raised this Jesus to life, and we are all witnesses of the fact. Exalted at the right hand of God, he has received from the Father the promised Holy Spirit and has poured out what you now see and hear" (Acts 2:32-33). True to form, God's manifestation on earth on the day of Pentecost was timed on the exact day of His Feast calendar's timing. That miraculous outpouring also marked the timing of the exaltation of the Son in heaven.

FROM "WITH" TO "IN"

When this new power in proclamation was being manifested in them, the surprised disciples began to remember that on the night before His crucifixion, Jesus had told them that a change of relationship was coming. He promised them a Comforter, the Spirit of truth—"for he lives <u>with</u> you and will be <u>in</u> you" (John 14:17.) A single preposition revealed the difference! The Spirit would soon indwell all those who receive Jesus. "All this I have spoken while still with you," He had said that night. "But the Counselor, the Holy Spirit, whom the Father will send in my name, will teach you all things and will remind you of everything I have said to you" (John 14:25-26). Forty days after His resurrection, just before His ascension from earth back to Heaven, Jesus had announced a new power coming to them, promising that, "you will receive power when the Holy Spirit comes on you; and you will be my witnesses in Jerusalem, and in all Judea and Samaria, and to the ends of the earth" (Acts 1:8).

FROM LAW TO GRACE

The "new covenant in my blood" would move God's relationship with believers from law to grace, from being engraved on stone to being written on hearts. As John would later summarize, "For the law was given through Moses; grace and truth came through Jesus Christ" (John 1:17). The Mosaic law was given as a mirror to show us our need for a Savior. Actually, the covenant of <u>promise</u>, made before the law, had itself been based all along on <u>grace</u>. As Paul explains, "For if the inheritance depends on the law, then it no longer depends on the promise; but God in His <u>grace</u> gave it to Abraham through a promise" (Galatians 3:18). Abraham didn't merit being given the promise; it was the gift of God's grace!

BUT...

Through the ages and right up to today, human nature rises up in pride, asking, "Can't I myself do something to merit God's favor?" A paraphrase of Scripture's clarification might be, *No. Forgiveness before God can only be received as a gift of grace to you, based on my Son's merit. Only sinless God-in-the-flesh could pay the enormous sin debt of the world. Had it not been our necessary solution, the Son's death on the cross would have had no ultimate meaning.*

ULTIMATE FULFILLMENT

Life in a fallen world is difficult. Jesus' Good News tells those who trust Him that they are covered by His sacrifice, and resourced by His indwelling Spirit, "until I come." We long for rest and peace, for the world's restoration, and for final fulfillment of God's promises. We also wonder, *How long, until You set things right? How long will it be till Your coming?* Let's search next for biblical clues to the longed-for reconciliation and restoration of all things that has yet to happen in God's promised future.

7 COVENANT COROLLARY:
Obedience or disobedience
Grace or judgment

✎ Leviticus 26 speaks of the seriousness of violating His covenant, and gives incentives and warnings related to responses to God's directives. When might you have sensed a tendency to disobedience, pride, or hostility toward God in your own life? Did you then, or do you regularly, appropriate the promises of I John 1:5-10?

✎ God's covenant with Abraham preceded the Mosaic covenant. So, the covenant of Promise precedes the Law, and is still in effect. Galatians 3:16-17 clarifies the Law's temporary role in bringing us to recognize our need for mercy. When or how did you recognize your need for mercy?

✎ Still today, we are tempted to revert to "the law" – trying to get acceptance with God on the basis of our good works. When or how might you have awakened to the promise of grace in humble dependence only on the work of the Savior?

Chapter 8
PROPHETIC VALIDATION

P eople are fascinated with the future. Consider fortune tellers, horoscopes, even fortune cookies. We wonder what will happen tomorrow, next week, or next year. We anticipate fears, and dream of future hopes. Jewish people for centuries have been repeating, "Next year in Jerusalem!" The Bible teaches us much about our past, applies to our present, and predicts our future. It's panoramic.

MATURE SEARCHING

A person's serious search for life's purpose leads to considering humanity's whole pilgrimage, i.e. getting the big picture. Little pieces fit into the whole. For instance, I had not really noticed the book of Ruth's connection to the Jubilee till well after our fiftieth anniversary, although I'd been reading the Bible for years. It had been a lovely "cameo" to me before, one of Scripture's unforgettable scenes, like Daniel in the lions' den, or David and Goliath. That's fine for childhood, but an adult level of understanding should take the Bible's whole story into account, seeing various scenes in relationship to the whole. We need to wake up and study up, to see the Scriptures comprehensively.

ANCIENT-TO-CURRENT RELATIONSHIPS

Of course, it is helpful to get a *geographical* overview of biblical history too. Maps are valuable. Travel to the land of the Bible is a precious gift. When we were in Israel for two weeks in 1988, before heading back to the States, my fellow travelers were awed by the ancient stones of Jerusalem. But I kept being focused on connecting with living stones—Jews and Arabs, but especially Black Jews of Ethiopia who had been secretly airlifted out of Sudan in 1984. I searched faces on the streets, hoping to discover some of them. Blank result. Eventually we went to the famous Wailing Wall, now a symbol of Jewish anguish and prayer. We stepped cautiously onto its public square, where Orthodox Jews nod their prayers facing the huge stones that make up the foundation of their ancient Temple. Jews are not allowed above, where Islam's Dome of the Rock now stands in the Temple's place, totally controlled by Muslim rule.

The Jewish community will never forget their loss of the Temple, Jerusalem, and their Promised Land at the hand of Rome. Their last stand, taken on the stark, high butte south of Jerusalem called "Masada," is etched painfully in their memory. That is where the last 900-some Jewish survivors took their own lives rather than be captured by Roman invaders about to storm their mountain retreat in AD 73. Israel's modern-day army recruits go through a ceremony which includes taking a vow: "Masada never again!" Amazingly, our moment of arrival at the Wailing Wall coincided with this commissioning taking place in the open square. On a series of wide steps on the opposite side facing the Wall, blocks of regiments were standing at attention facing the famous foundation stones. Having been attacked repeatedly, Israel requires all young people to do two years of military training, for preparedness. We had not taken into account that Jews were returning to Israel from all over the world. These regiments included blocks of alien immigrants who had made *aliya* to Israel. To our amazement, there in front of us stood a whole regiment of coffee-with-cream-colored soldiers—Ethiopia's "Black Jews"!

These were sons and daughters of the Falasha community in Ethiopia who had dreamed for centuries of "next year in Jerusalem." David prophesied that because of the Temple at Jerusalem, "Ethiopia hastens to stretch out her hands to God" (Psalm 68:31 RSV). The Queen of Sheba had "stretched out" hers in the 900's BC, and the Ethiopian eunuch from Queen Candace's court had done so shortly after the Resurrection. An Ethiopian Orthodox presence has been extant in Israel up to our own day. We visited the Ethiopian Orthodox church in Jerusalem, which is located right across the pavement from the Church of the Holy Sepulcher. The actual presence of those Ethiopian Jewish and Christian communities in the Holy City drew prophetic history together for me—like the ribs of an accordion squeezed tight.

One time on a flight home to the States, our plane connection required an overnight in Rome. That brief touch brought us to the actual cobblestones where Paul walked, to the very Coliseum where early Christians died. We in the New World know little of these historical centerpieces. Such encounters widen our grasp of history in a way that stretches life out beyond our own times. We sense something of the infinite.

THIRST FOR THE WHOLE

As I consider these experiences, I realize why I was drawn to the study of the LORD's feasts. I wanted to know how history looks from above, panoramically, from the One who knows the end from the beginning. The feasts' stipulations act like a picture book that puts the year's ceremonial happenings into practicable terms. When celebrated then, or even now, they expand and brighten the community's life. Eschatologically, the progression of the feasts spans history.

GOD'S GOAL

Reviewing various levels of meaning found in the feasts, three viewpoints are agricultural, historical, and spiritual interpretations. However, we haven't specifically focused yet on the fourth level, the prophetic. It will be valuable to look at God's feasts from the standpoint of eschatology before finishing our Jubilee journey. God gave the Hebrews a concept of time that moves in a linear way toward a goal, not cyclical like eastern religions. The ultimate Jubilee represents that goal, and the feasts progress along the linear line of history toward that climax. To focus on feasts without keeping their ultimate fulfillment in mind is to miss the point of the prophetic level of God's teaching methods.

FALSE PROPHETS INOCULATE

But why is it that in most of Christendom today, parables and sermons and prayers are acceptable, but biblical prophecy is an avoided topic? The Old Testament books of the prophets and New Testament prophetic passages make up as much as a fourth of biblical revelation. So why is prophecy scoffed at? One cause is the enemy's ongoing disinformation campaign.

The agent of rebellion and blinding works against humanity's understanding of God's goal. Satan uses false prophets and presumptive prophecies proven wrong to nudge people to "throw out the baby with the bathwater," so to speak. Scripture makes it clear that prophecies are to be carefully tested. Their authenticity is shown clearly by whether the prophecy proves true to life —and not just metaphorically, but actually. God stated the test:

> You may say to yourselves, "How can we know when a message has not been spoken by the LORD?" If what a prophet proclaims in the name of the LORD does not take place or come true, that is a message the LORD has not spoken. That prophet has spoken presumptively. Do not be afraid of him (Deuteronomy 18:21-22).

In our times, numerous false prophecies dating the return of Christ have proven untrue. Since charlatans have "cried wolf" repeatedly, it has become natural to dismiss the whole subject.

LINEAR HISTORY AND THE ETERNAL NOW

God teaches that history is moving toward the accomplishment of His intention. Jubilees foreshadow that goal. Finally, all that has been wrong will be put right. His covenant community will come home, be redeemed, and be free! God Himself proclaims the Jubilee. The Feasts of the LORD demonstrate progression toward a goal:

- ✓ Feast of the Sabbath at the peak of the week.
- ✓ Feast of Tabernacles at the close of the year.
- ✓ "Sabbath rest" for the land the seventh year.
- ✓ 50th year recalibration of society at the close of seven cycles of seven.

These all speak of progression toward final blessings in time, so would it not be reasonable to ask, *might they suggest final blessing in eternity?* Similarly, Jubilee clue words given to Isaiah in his time, but also applicable to the future, can be recognized in his passages on the restoration of Israel. For instance, consider this one already referred to in chapter 4 (p. 50):

> This is what the LORD says: "<u>In the time of my favor</u> I will answer you, and in the day of salvation I will help you. I will keep you and will make you to be a covenant for the people, to <u>restore the land</u> and to <u>reassign its desolate inheritances</u>, to say to the <u>captives, 'Come out,'</u> and to <u>those in darkness, 'Be free!'</u>" (Isaiah 49:8-9)

Eternity does not move according to the cadence of time! God's reconciliation of all things, including our own restoration, can be accomplished with just a word. He created the world with a word; He can re-create it with a word. Jesus, God in the flesh, kept doing the same: just a word to the storm, just a word to the demon, just a word to dead Lazarus.

LITERAL TRUTH

Jesus' miracles were noticeably physical in nature—wine, food, storms, healings, resurrections. They were therefore provable or disprovable. Physicality carried through in the Apostolic writings. As the Gospel of John insists, "The Word became flesh" (John 1:11). "This is how you can recognize the Spirit of God: Every spirit that acknowledges that Jesus Christ has come in the flesh is from God" (I John 4:2). Spiritualization of actualities can detour plain faith. Did the allegorical interpretation of prophecy in the early ages neutralize its prophetic meanings and expectations? Did it substitute a kingdom on earth for the Kingdom of heaven? Would the Church or the King of Kings bring in the Kingdom of righteousness?

DISMISSAL OF PROPHECY

Prophecy is avoided by many, but as noted above it makes up a huge swath of Scripture. To ignore it seems an insult to God, for it is His method of warning, encouraging, predicting, and verifying His truth. For example, prophecies of Isaiah stretch across time remarkably, over and over warning that God's righteous judgment on Israel's unfaithfulness would be executed, but always giving hope for future restoration. Long before the Babylonian captivity, the Spirit of God through Isaiah predicts coming judgment as well as the eventual decree of Cyrus the Persian, who will release the captive Hebrews to return and rebuild Jerusalem. (See Isaiah 44:28; 45:1.)

THE CHURCH'S HISTORICAL DECEPTION

In addition to the damage false predictions have done to people's confidence in prophecy, God's enemy also has blinded the Church's attention to huge portions of Scripture. Obviously, much of the Old Testament prophecies are "Jewish," since they are focused on the past and future expectations of God's covenant people. In the early centuries, when Rome largely took over the faith, Jewishness was forcibly washed out of church doctrine and practice, including the lunar calendar, the Sabbath, and God's "appointed feasts unto the LORD." New constructs in line with Gentile thinking were substituted, and a new calendar was created. The Church assumed it had superseded Israel and had absorbed the promises for Israel into a Gentile-ized Christianity. The Spirit's warnings about relational principles between Jews and Gentiles, made clear in Romans 9-11, were set aside.

The present-day emergence of the nation of Israel has come as a shock to most of Christendom. The flowering around the world of congregations of Messianic Jewish believers in Jesus (as having been and still being the Messiah) comes as a surprise. These developments are perplexing in light of skewed assumptions that Israel was "finished." Suddenly, all those chapters promising the final restoration of Israel are coming into view. These fulfillments may be a harbinger of the "time of the Gentiles" coming to a close. (See Luke 21:24.) They may signal the Messiah's soon return.

FALSE PRESUPPOSITIONS CAUSE AN IMPASSE

Furthermore, age-long dismissal of "Jewishness" has led to a dangerous impasse among Christians over the Israeli/Palestinian situation today. Christendom generally seems to have forgotten God's firm pronouncement that the land of Israel belongs to Him (Leviticus 25:23), and seems to disregard His having "leased" the promised land to the covenant people through whom the Messiah was to come, and to which Christ promised to return the second time. The typical modern assessment of the Middle East situation is based on a God-ignoring, unbiblical, and secular understanding of recent history. In a fallen world so graphically imprinted by the Holocaust, Europe's guilty gesture allowing Jews to escape to Israel created still another displacement chapter in our broken world's history. The age-long animosity between half-brothers (Isaac and Ishmael) has been mightily used by the enemy of God to lethally damage both Jews and Palestinians. Their struggle is dividing the worldwide Church, as well.

THEREFORE, A "PERFECT STORM"

With biblical roots nearly forgotten or denied, deceptions on many levels face today's globally-focused generation. Anti-Semitism is rising rampant in Europe and emerging strident in America, too. Add to this today's surprising, world-wide emergence of a pandemic, and a thinking person who understands the Scriptures can hardly avoid feeling it is time to be wide awake. We may be living at a deeply significant time of history, one that darkens with judgment but also glows with expectation. It's not a time to keep our heads in the sand, or be obsessed with threats to our health and wealth. It's a time to call people to examine the prophetic passages in the Bible, so that they can investigate for themselves what God has said about the future. It's time to get serious personally about the deeper questions of life. Figuratively speaking, it's time for the Church corporately to remember the Feast of Trumpet's blasts announcing, "time to confess sins against God and man," in light of the inevitable judgments connected with the future Day of Atonement. Jewish and Gentile believers need to reassess our obedience to what God ordains to be required before the Jubilee. In what roles and relationships have we failed? What reconciliations cry for attention?

PROOF ON TRIAL

God's true prophets revealed His perspective to the nation, sometimes through dramatic real-life metaphors. Even in their pronouncements of judgment, hope of restoration shines through. Prophets were <u>forth</u>-tellers of God's message to His people. They also were <u>fore</u>-tellers of events either soon to happen, or in the far future, or both. God tells Habakkuk, "For the revelation awaits an appointed time. It speaks of the end and will not prove false. Though it lingers, wait for it" (Habakkuk 2:3).

Scripture repeatedly gives us examples of God's control over history through being the only One who could know the future. Repeatedly, although the LORD would give His prophet a message, the prophet was usually disbelieved, resisted, or even martyred for stating what was true. Nevertheless, God's prediction eventually did come to pass—thus vindicating the authenticity of the messenger and the message, but sometimes after his death.

PAST EXAMPLES?

➢ Abraham is told he will not inherit the Promised Land for 400 years. Their exodus from slavery and move into Canaan happened 400 years later.

➢ Jeremiah is told that Judah's captivity in Babylon will last 70 years; Daniel believes it, Cyrus allows it, and the 70-year prediction proves true.

➢ Isaiah's 53rd chapter predicted detail after detail of the suffering of the Lamb of God, and each detail matches what the Savior experienced at the crucifixion some 700 years later.

➢ Jesus keeps stating an impossibility: that He will be killed, and in three days will arise from the grave. This happens. If He had not actually come back alive, the Messiah's resurrection would not have become the watershed of history!

FUTURE EXPECTATIONS

Notice that Jesus gave us a huge body of prophetic warnings and encouragements in the Gospels and Revelation. Having already passed the test of His authenticity, there is no reason to doubt that His predictions about the future will come true.

CLUE OF THE EIGHTH DAY

Rehearsed weekly, yearly, and at the half-century mark, the feasts immersed Israelites in His prophetic sequence toward a completion. As we look back at the whole system, the Spirit can give us eyes to see the pattern and discern something of God's goal. He gave "future" clues. For instance, at the end of the yearly feasts, at the end of the Feast of Tabernacles, a strange addition is ordained. They are commanded, "So beginning with the fifteenth day of the seventh month, after you have gathered the crops of the land, celebrate the festival to the LORD for seven days; the first day is a day of rest, and the *eighth* day also is a day of rest" (Leviticus 23:39). What is an "eighth day" if any week has seven? Why would a seven-day feast add an eighth day? Might it be a clue to something new, something beyond?

CLUE OF THE FIFTIETH DAY

At the end of the seven feasts celebrated seven times, one more day is added, the Jubilee. Is this day added to 49 years a similar clue foreshadowing eternity? Furthermore, does the Jubilee encompass what would be consistent with eternity? Would its elements display what people might hope for, after physical death? Rest, redemption, reconciliation, restoration?

MINERS' REWARD

History, covenants, prophecy, feasts, Jubilee—these are pages in the Biblical Manual as God recalibrated the Hebrew community's lives at Mount Sinai, after their Egyptian bondage. Thinking we moderns are beyond all that, and forgetting our debt to the Messianic community, many rarely turn to the biblical feast pages. What a loss! God's Word is like a mine with many veins. Those who dig deeply into the feast vein discover gems whose many facets gleam. The Jubilee glows with eternity's light!

8 PROPHETIC VALIDATION:
God's method of proof

✎ How does Jesus' use of Isaiah 61:1-3 to identify Himself help you trust the reliability of Isaiah's prophecies? How do Isaiah's prophecies from 52:13-15 through chapter 53 accurately mirror the Savior's suffering?

✎ Jesus' predictions of His resurrection proved true. (See Mark 9:31-33; Luke 9:21-22; Matthew 26:52-56; and John 13:33.) His resurrection was the fulcrum of His disciples' witness to the world. As you think about your own witness to others, how centrally does the Savior's resurrection fit into your narrative?

✎ How seriously do you expect Jesus' promises of His return? (Matthew 16:27; Luke 17:22-37; John 14:1-4; Acts 1:10-11; Revelation 1:7-8; 22:7, 12, 20 and more.) What emotions does that expectation cause within you?

Chapter 9
NOT UNTIL

Our look at the Jubilee through a prophetic lens leads us to the obvious question: "Then, when will the ultimate Jubilee finally happen?" Or in other terms, "When will Jesus' promised return issue in the Jubilee?" "When will God's goal for history be reached?"

Consider that all over the world, as believers celebrate Jesus' Last Supper, we hear the words:

> This is the new covenant in my blood; do this whenever you drink it, in remembrance of me. For whenever you eat this bread and drink this cup, you proclaim the Lord's death until he comes (I Corinthians 11:25-26).

Until! That's where we are; we're living in the "until" period of history, moving toward God's goal!

WHEN?

Jesus followers have been asking "When?" ever since the Incarnation. Right after the Lord's resurrection, His disciples were asking it. Being citizens of a nation who hoped for a political Messiah, they did not yet grasp God's world-wide intention. It would take the arrival of the Holy Spirit to reveal their interim assignment. On the day of the Lord's ascension, they were still thinking of fulfillment in earthly terms. They asked the risen Messiah, "Lord, are you at this time going to restore the kingdom to Israel?" (Acts 1:6) They still were expecting that the Messianic climax would establish the kingdom of Israel. But Jesus was bringing in the Kingdom of God! He had to refocus them on their world-wide task, not the timing:

He said to them, "It is not for you to know the times or dates the Father has set by his own authority. But you will receive power when the Holy Spirit comes to you; and you will be my witnesses in Jerusalem, and in all Judea and Samaria, and to the ends of the earth" (Acts 1:7-8).

They trusted their Lord, and so they did begin spreading the Good News throughout the wider world.

UNTIL WHEN, JERUSALEM?

Jesus did predict the timing of His return in relationship to Israel. That last week before the cross, Jesus told the disciples that the Temple would go down, and their question was, "Tell us, when will these things happen?" (See Matthew 24:3, Mark 13:4, Luke 21:7.) In the last four days between the supposedly "triumphal" entry of the Messiah and His crucifixion, the Lord poured out His last parables, prophecies, and promises, but also His woes upon Israel's corrupt religious leadership. We're reminded again that Jesus cried out,

Oh Jerusalem, Jerusalem, you who kill the prophets and stone those sent to you, how often I have longed to gather your children together, as a hen gathers her chicks under her wings, but you were not willing. Look, your house is left to you desolate. For I tell you, you will not see me again until you say, "Blessed is he who comes in the name of the Lord" (Matthew 23:37-39).

At His departure, Jesus' concerns were to prepare the followers who received Him, but to warn those who rejected Him. The Redeemer's predictions in Matthew 24 and 25 are sometimes called "the little Apocalypse." They proceed from the destruction of the Temple (which happened 40 years later), to signs of the end of the age, to the final judgment that will divide "sheep" and "goats." He did reveal a time-connected clue. Predicting the future, He said, "Jerusalem will be trampled on by the Gentiles _until the times of the Gentiles are fulfilled_" (Luke 21:24).

UNTIL WHEN, GENTILES?

After Pentecost opened up the message of salvation to the whole world, New Testament letters revealed more about the Lord's promised return. Although a hater of Christians, the Pharisee Paul suddenly met the risen Christ. _Yeshua_ assigned him to be the apostle to the Gentiles. Yet he kept yearning for his own people's salvation, as Romans 10 so poignantly expresses. Paul speaks of a time period using the "until" term: "Israel has experienced a hardening in part _until the full number of Gentiles has come in_" (Romans 11:26).

"GENTILE-IZATION" REPERCUSSIONS

Although the first believers in Jesus were nearly all Jewish, people in Gentile nations began to believe and eventually far outnumbered the original community. The church slowly became "Gentile-ized." The watershed Jerusalem Council (Acts 15) bowed to the Spirit and accepted Gentiles as brother believers, without "becoming Jews" (i.e. being circumcised, keeping the law). In contrast, starting in the 300s AD, the Gentile church would only accept Jews if they "became Gentiles." Can you imagine what it meant to the original covenant community to be forbidden to keep the sign of their covenant, the Sabbath, or not be allowed to celebrate the Passover? Christendom rejected its Jewish moorings. It forbade a Jew to be a Jewish Christian. Right down to today, the Church has inherited this illogical conundrum.

AMILLENNIAL REPERCUSSIONS

Christendom's generally amillennial conception of prophecy grew out of Augustine's allegorical interpretation of Scripture. The prophetic reign of Christ on earth (Revelation 20:4-5) became a case in point. If we dismiss the Messiah's "millennium" (1,000 years) on earth, how many other Scriptures might be considered metaphorical rather than plainly physical? If His return were not to be physical, might His resurrection not have been literally physical either? Paul anticipated this false conclusion in his famous passage on Christ's resurrection in I Corinthians 15:12-18. The risen Messiah anticipated it too, the night of His resurrection. Not to be thought nonphysical, as a ghost or vision, He purposefully asked for fish to eat in front of His disciples! (Luke 24:40-42)

BEGGING YOUR PARDON, DEAR READER...

I realize that some of this book's readers, and many of my own good friends, take an amillennial view of the prophetic future, admittedly the majority opinion. Disagreement on secondary doctrines like prophecy need not isolate brothers and sisters in the faith from each other. I've tried to progressively explain where I am coming from, so that even if a reader may disagree, it will be helpful to understand how people have arrived at different conclusions and convictions.

"REPLACEMENT" REPERCUSSIONS

What has been the result of reversals away from Romans 9-11 teachings about "root and branch" relationships? Might the dismissal of God's promises to Israel (thinking them absorbed into the Church) have de-railed the progression of the Gospel? Teaching that Israel was finished and has been replaced by the church became an underlying false assumption that we now call "replacement theology." This viewpoint and accompanying attitudes contributed to persecutions and atrocities toward Jews over the centuries. They starkly attest to tragic results right up to the Holocaust in our times. Now, only eighty-some years later, virulent anti-Semitism is emerging in Europe again, and even in the States. Satan's determination to destroy the Messianic people is perpetual. Christians are challenged to admit compliance with atrocities in the past, and rethink where Israel fits into God's plan. Along with empathizing with the Palestinian's tragic predicament, we must face how to honor and protect the Lord's chosen people today, the people of the patriarchs and prophets from whom Gentiles received the Word of God, and the whole world's Savior.

UNTIL WHEN, CHURCH?

The Church is now living in the waiting mode—in the assignment phase of Jesus' commission to reach the world. (See Acts 1:8.) "The times of the Gentiles" are sometimes called "the age of grace" or "the church age." To review, ever since the 4th feast, Pentecost, was fulfilled, we are in the gap between the fulfillment of the three spring feasts during the Incarnation, and the unfulfilled fall feasts at harvest time. Prophetically, now is the season of planting, before the 5th feast's trumpets warn the need for Atonement, the 6th; after which the "ingathering" of the 7th feast can be celebrated. Remember that the spring feast celebrations spanned less than two weeks, the timing of which the Savior's passion and resurrection fulfilled. Celebration of the fall feasts took less than a month, meaning God's time-matched fulfillments at "closing time" may be quick.

Jesus gave His disciples a commission. It would seem that the conclusion of our assignment could depend upon our obedience: "And this gospel of the kingdom will be preached in the whole world as a testimony to all nations, and then the end will come" (Matthew 24:14). The early church "turned the world upside down" (Acts 17:6) and dotted over the centuries there have been historic endeavors to reach the pagan world. Yet much of Christendom has wandered in its own wilderness of unfaithfulness and mere tradition. In recent times, bold and determined initiatives have been launched to reach the nations (i.e. the Gentiles), and by now a whole new wave of multi-ethnic ambassadors of the Kingdom are presently spreading out across the world.

Examples? Consider the following initiatives in connection to Yeshua/Jesus' commission to "make disciples of all nations." (See Matthew 28:19-20 plus Matthew 24:14.)

➢ **Wycliffe Bible Translators** have been laboring over languages with no alphabet; technology is speeding up the process; new ways for reaching illiterate oral societies are being employed.

> The huge project known as the **Jesus Film** dramatizes the book of Luke, dubbing in each ethnic group's voices speaking in their people's tongue. Campus Crusade's (Cru) Jesus Film leadership reports that as of 2020, this oral and visual depiction has been recorded into 1,857 languages, so that 97% of the world's population can watch the docudrama on the life of Christ in their mother tongue.

> Consider the prolific mobilizing effect of the U.S. Center's **Mission Perspectives** courses and other similar initiatives.

> Perhaps most significant, let us be aware of the tidal wave of maturing non-Western missionary outreaches now fanning out over the globe.

BUT WHAT ABOUT UNBELIEVING ISRAEL?

With Jews scattered all over the world for centuries and the Holy Land languishing in relative barrenness, prophecies centered on the restoration of Israel and Jerusalem seemed impossible to fulfill. Centuries passed. Then less than a hundred years ago, Hitler's "final solution" to rid the world of Jews resulted in the Holocaust's inhuman genocide of God's covenant people. Prayed for by earlier British Zionists, and partly because of Europe's sense of guilt, a movement surfaced that led to allowing Jews to emigrate to their ancient homeland. Suddenly, with the biblical location for Jesus' return restored, Bible-believing Christians hoped the time of His promised return might be close. For those who had yearned for the Lord's coming, 1948 was an indelible year! On the other hand, most of Christendom had considered Israel finished and the Church to have permanently superseded and replaced the covenant people. Prophetic promises of restoration had been ignored or interpreted metaphorically for centuries, and concrete fulfillments were not expected. For much of Christendom, 1948's "birth of a nation in a day" was either incidental, or perplexing.

MY 1948 EXPERIENCE

In August of 1948, two of us from Sunflower Girls State were chosen to represent Kansas at Girls Nation in Washington DC. Our delegation of a hundred young women was received in the Rose Garden of the White House. We each shook the hand of President Harry Truman. Raised in Republican Kansas, I secretly resented the President's being a Democrat. Little did I know, nor could I yet realize, the significance of the American president's declaration of authentication three months before, on May 14, 1948, recognizing Israel's nationhood. The covenant people, scattered for 2000 years, being reconstituted! Israel came onto the stage of history again. In fact, the world has been reeling around Jerusalem ever since. By biblical standards, we live in prophetic times.

THE SIGNIFICANCE OF ABSENCE

What does 1948 signify on the biblical calendar? In my search through recent books on Christian history, I've noticed the glaring absence of "Israel" as a major topic in the index. Why this absence? Doesn't the whole Old Testament focus on Israel, beginning with the role of God's promises to Abraham's family as God's chosen vessel to bring forth the Seed who would be the whole world's Savior? Yet today's attitude toward Christian history regularly seems blind to the biblical promises to Israel which the Scriptures predict will come to pass in the last days. Alas, both covenant communities seem to have blind spots. While unbelieving Jews keep Isaiah 53 under wraps today, many churches seem to keep eschatology under wraps even now. Why? Overlooked truths would upset theologies long held and interrupt power structures long in place. But where does blindness really come from? At the root, God's enemy has largely succeeded in blinding God's covenant people, separating Christendom from her Jewish roots, and dividing the Church into theological/political camps.

ROMANS CHAPTERS 9 TO 11

God's promises to Israel—through whose Seed the LORD promised to bless the world—have not been completed. A Hebrew of the tribe of Benjamin, Paul always went to his people first, and kept grieving over his own countrymen's spiritual blindness. In Romans 9 and 10 he agonizes over that concern. In chapter 11, he warns Gentile believers not to "boast over the root" into whom they have been grafted as unnatural branches. "If you do, consider this: you do not support the root, but the root supports you" (Romans 11:18). It is telling that the 9th to 11th chapters of Romans are regularly either overlooked or kept quiet in much of Christendom.

MY BONDING WITH A DAUGHTER OF ABRAHAM

Considering myself of the "branch," my own respect for the "root" people drew me to a young Jewish fellow English teacher in my department at our university. A secular Jew and a *Sabra* (having served in the military), she had immigrated to the States to make a life for herself as a widow with two children.

We developed a close friendship. The summer Charlie and I traveled to Israel, she also returned there to visit her mother in Tel Aviv. We overlapped in Tel Aviv and the next week in Jerusalem.

Charlie and I heard about a late-night Messianic meeting at the King David Hotel, and she agreed to come along. In the 1980s only a fledgling number of Jews recognized that Jesus really was and is the Messiah. The meeting's grand piano, cello, and violin music were magnificent. Teaching was all in Hebrew. I yearned for my friend to be hearing the Good News in her own heart language.

While people were filing out, she grabbed a young female dressed in the attire of a military trainee, and drilled her with questions.

"Who was your grandfather?" she demanded.

"An Orthodox priest—in Australia," the soldier responded.

"Well, who was your father?"

"An atheist—in Israel."

"So, who are you?"

The answer came without hesitation: "I'm a completed Jew!" Stunned, our friend asked no more questions.

Munching on falafel and hummus at a midnight café that night, I asked what most impressed her about the meeting, hoping the Hebrew language had done its work. She paused to consider, and then answered, "It was seeing Jews and Arabs sitting next to each other, nothing I've ever seen before. How can that be?" I had been hoping she'd get the biblical content, but she was seeing the effect of the Gospel's good news. I longed for her to realize what Scripture tells us is the reason why Jews and non-Jews can accept each other:

But now in Christ Jesus you who once were far away
have been brought near through the blood of Christ. For
he himself is our peace, who has made the two one and
has destroyed the barrier, the dividing wall of hostility,
by abolishing it in his flesh. His purpose was to create
in himself one new man, out of the two, thus making
peace, and in this one body to reconcile both of them to
God through the cross. For through him we both have
access to the Father by one Spirit (Ephesians 2:14-18).

Evidently the sight of that curiously mixed congregation
communicated more to our dear friend than words did. She
was seeing truth in the flesh. Within the Messianic community,
descendants of both Isaac and Ishmael were bowing to the
Lord's sovereignty in having chosen one branch of Abraham's
family out of which to bring the Messiah. In that acquiescence,
they were being freed from the competitive jealousy and hatred
that stalks the Middle East.

WIDER IMPLICATIONS

Will the family of Abraham reconcile? How wonderful that
would be! Jesus' work of reconciliation is the only "peace plan"
that can heal the animosity between the two sons of Abraham.
Their enmity goes back a long way. Genesis recounts the life
story of Abraham and Isaac, the son of the Messianic line. We
learn that infertile Sarah attempted to get an heir through a
surrogate mother. Hagar bore Abraham's first son, Ishmael,
thirteen years before Sarah miraculously gave birth to Isaac.
The jealousy between Isaac and Ishmael still festers in the
Middle East.

The God of Abraham, Isaac, and Jacob made a sovereign
choice that carefully superintended the family line through
which to redeem the world. In Genesis 21 God states, "It is

through Isaac that your offspring will be reckoned. I will make the son of the maidservant into a nation also, because he is your offspring." In response to Abraham's deep love for his firstborn son, God makes a promise: "And as for Ishmael, I have heard you. I will surely bless him; I will make him fruitful and will greatly increase his number. He will be the father of twelve rulers, and I will make him a great nation. But my covenant I will establish with Isaac" (Genesis 17:20). God's love is impartial, but His redemptive plan is specific.

WATCHING THE MESSIANIC MOVEMENT

We came back to America from our two weeks in Israel with two stereotype-shattering books written by an Israeli named David Stern: *Restoring the Jewishness of the Gospel* and *A Messianic Jewish Manifesto*. Our little window on the beginnings of the Messianic movement in Jerusalem awakened me to its implications in relationship to the Lord's return, and caused me to keep watching the movement develop. In 1988, I was seeing Jerusalem's Jewish believers in the Messiah as first fruits beginning to sprout up. Two decades later I would see the movement blossoming on American soil.

BREAKTHROUGH IN AMERICA

Since our memorable evening in Jerusalem, the Messianic movement has multiplied into scores of Messianic congregations in Israel, the States, and around the world. In the "Jesus People" era in California, many young Jews languishing in the drug culture miraculously came to *Yeshua*/Jesus, often through the witness of Gentile Christians. They eventually discovered each other and became a movement. By now Jewish believers have produced scores of books witnessing to having discovered the true identity of *Yeshua*/Jesus. *The Messianic Times* magazine includes pages listing Messianic Jewish congregations over the world. Those in the United States take three pages to list. In 2020, twenty-five Messianic congregations are listed in Israel, six in Jerusalem itself. Consider what this breakthrough could mean in light of Jesus' words as He wept over Jerusalem. Jewish believers in Jerusalem in our own day are actually acclaiming Jesus, saying "Blessed is he who comes in the name of the Lord."

MY WEEK OF JEWISH IMMERSION

The MJAA (Messianic Jewish Association of America) is probably the largest association of Jewish Christians living in the States. Actually, they don't use the older term "Hebrew Christians," but prefer now to be called "Messianic Jews." (Paul Liberman's book, *Don't Call me Christian* explains why they chose that term. In their Jewish community's eyes, "Christian" has treasonous implications—since it designates their people's persecutors and annihilators over the last 2000 years.)

In 2016, I visited Mechanicsburg, Pennsylvania, where our family friend is a professor at Messiah College. It was the week of the annual MJAA Convention. Messiah College had a name and size that was chosen decades ago as a fitting venue for the MJAA'S yearly "Messiah Conference." I was one of a few Gentiles alongside about a thousand Jewish believers in Jesus. Whole families came. I had been invited to take part in their "Book Night," because of our book, *The Messiah Mystery*, and my trilogy of studies published by Olive Press. What a privilege that night to be among Messianic Jewish authors whose books testify to having found Jesus to be the Messiah after all!

That week was an immersion in Jewish culture—eating kosher foods, hearing shofars joyously blown, watching Davidic dancing, attending various seminars, joining the whole community's nightly preaching services, and experiencing their *Shabbat*. The evening meetings featured worship—music often in that haunting Middle Eastern minor key—led by groups from Israel and Ukraine, as well as the States. The MJAA's Joseph Project raised thousands for relief work in Israel. Israeli and American leaders spoke. The final message was given by Jonathan Cahn, a Messianic Jewish rabbi who is becoming a well-known speaker and writer.

GENTILE BELIEVERS AWAKENING TO THE ROLE OF ISRAEL

Observers today point to Israel's 1948 "becoming a nation in a day" as deeply significant in terms of setting the scene for the Messiah's promised return. Prophecies yet to be fulfilled revolve around Israel and Jerusalem. Gentiles do well to keep God's eternal promises to Abraham, Isaac, and Jacob in mind. Today's convergence of fast-multiplying signs of biblical proportions lead us to consider whether the world's writhing may be signaling our nearness to the Day so often pointed to in Scripture.

Bible readers have been tempted to "set a date" based on the presumed Jubilee year pattern. But no! *Yeshua*/Jesus stated that He would come at an unexpected time, a time known only to the Father. He warned against presumption, but urged His own to be trusting, waiting, watching, and ready. Meanwhile, His *ecclesia* is to "proclaim the Lord's death, until He comes."

AGAIN, A TIE WITH RUTH

Understanding Hebrew often reveals deeper meanings to Scriptural passages. Jonathan Cahn's *The Book of Mysteries* explains what most Gentiles would easily miss without reading the Bible in light of Hebrew language and culture. We looked at the Book of Ruth in Chapter 6. A cultural Jewish tie is that the book of Ruth was customarily read aloud during Israel's feast of *Shavuot,* Pentecost, the feast day at which 2,000 years ago the Spirit of God spoke God's message of salvation in multiple languages to the Jewish diaspora who had come to Jerusalem from the wider Gentile world. Three thousand that day believed!

The underlying significance of Ruth and Boaz' Gentile/Jewish union makes us wonder about the long stretch of waiting for the world's Kinsman Redeemer to return. The delay highlights how Satan has derailed the relationships the two communities were to enjoy. We ponder today's impasse between Israel and the Church. In *The Book of Mysteries* (Day 161), Jonathan Cahn views Naomi as representing Israel. He sees true believers (called the church) to be Ruth, Naomi's adopted Gentile daughter. Here is how Jonathan sees it:

> At the end of the story Ruth bears a child who becomes the blessing of Naomi's life. So, through Naomi comes Ruth's redemption, and through Ruth comes Naomi's blessing…. So those who are blessed with salvation are blessed through Israel and become part of Israel. They are Ruth…and Israel is their Naomi. And so it is only when Ruth blesses Naomi…and Naomi blesses Ruth…that the circle…and the story…will be complete.

Might Naomi and Ruth's mutual appreciation, union, and blessing be emerging at this time in history? Perhaps believing

Israelites and believing Gentiles will growingly recognize their mutual unifier, *Yeshua*/Jesus, Israel's and the world's Kinsman Redeemer.

"UNTIL HE COMES"—GETTING CLOSER?

Considering Jesus' "until" word to unbelieving Jerusalem, and His "until" commission to believers, today's conditions may signal prophetic completions beginning to fall into place. The tribes and nations are increasingly being reached. Messianic believers in Jesus are discovering Jesus to be alive, and truly Israel's Messiah. Many of them have written testimonial biographies, and some of their writers helpfully analyze today's situation in light of prophecy. (The biblical test for authenticity still applies, and not all that is put forth is reliable.) The Bible cannot be added to, but contemporary events can be explored in the light of prophecy, and testimonies can continue to demonstrate the reality of the faith in any generation.

Who would have thought that in this decade a Messianic Jewish rabbi named Jonathan Cahn would be asked to be the keynote speaker twice at the Capitol's Presidential Prayer Breakfast? His books have sold by the millions. In *The Oracle*, he explores historical events in the last two centuries related to Israel and the United States. In light of what? Of significant happenings in what he perceives to have been the Hebrew calendar's years of the biblical Jubilee! Is that not interesting?

9 NOT UNTIL: When will God's goal for history be reached?

✎ Not until what, did Jesus say to Jerusalem about His return? Matthew 23: 27-29

✎ Not until what, did Jesus say about His return to the disciples? Matthew 24:14

✎ Not until what, is explained about the Gentiles, related to Israel's "hardening" of heart? Romans 11:25

✎ Not until when, will believers celebrate the Lord's Supper? I Corinthians 11:25-26

Chapter 10
ENTER COVID-19

Back when life was the old normal, during our many Wellspring Fellowship years, the farm that our neighbors turned over to the Lord's use hosted a fun variety of activities. The old red Swihart barn, after emptied of hay, became a great event venue with an improvised kitchen at one end, and at the other, a little stage for "Down on the Farm" fun nights. A rustic prayer chapel in the woods was our first addition—a tall gazebo put together out of old storm windows, around a stone-laid floor and a rough altar rock. Planks of dilapidated old farm sheds metamorphosed into a two-room cabin, with its own outhouse, no less. An old granary with loft was converted into a family cabin. Tents provided additional guest housing to our own homes' bedrooms during weekend Family Life Retreats, Spiritual Dynamics Conferences, and more meditative personal getaways called "Quiet Retreats."

THE CELEBRATION THAT MUSHROOMED

Holidays—Jewish and Christian—inspired all sorts of gatherings. One experiment started with three families along our Kitten Creek Road, then grew into a Wellspring event. It was so appreciated that the cast and back-up staff eventually expanded to include people from many local faith communities and became a yearly Christmas pageant offered to the town.

The first weekend of December, the farm is transformed in the darkness of night into another time and place, becoming the "Bethlehem Revisited" walk-through panoramic story of Christ. Visitors from the local area and surrounding towns walk over the paths and hills of the farm led by narrating guides who are carrying lanterns and robed in biblical-time costumes. Firepits at the various stations offer respite from the cold. Starlight, live animals, and sometimes snow, add to the sense of reality.

The pilgrimage begins with four pauses to hear prophecies of the coming Messiah from Old Testament prophets... moves up through Joseph and Mary's home in Nazareth (the two-room cabin)... on with Mary seated on a live donkey... encountering Roman soldiers mounted on horseback... on through the marketplace stalls (children love playing the part of vendors selling—and snitching—freshly baked loaves of bread)... past Bethlehem's "no vacancy" inn... hearing the angelic choir on the hill above shepherds with their flock of live sheep... on to the barn's lower hay shed, where the newborn baby Jesus (a real infant) lies in the stable... on to the pillars of the Jerusalem Temple... hearing testimonies from people the Lord healed... on to the cross... and finally, the empty tomb!

The Bethlehem Revisited pageant keeps being requested annually, and at this point (with no advertising except word of mouth), draws nearly 3,000 people each December. The project requires a cast and support staff of over 200 from the local community, not counting twenty-some live animals! More on this pageant's story is told in the last section of Nancy Swihart's memoir, *Searching for the Sacred on Kitten Creek*.

RESURRECTION MORNINGS

Even before the Christmas pageant developed, Wellspring fellowship families had begun using the "tomb" to gather around before dawn on Resurrection morning. A huge stone was added beside the cave's entrance. This old root cellar may have been where the original farm family ran to long ago during Kansas tornados. My dear Charlie's custom on the Saturday before Easter was to get out his old baritone from high school days and practice haltingly with no "lip" in shape. Then, when thirty or more Wellspringers gathered at the tomb before dawn on Resurrection morning, he'd blast out "Up from the Grave He Arose!" Getting sleepy-eyed children up that early is hard, but their reward was a delicious breakfast in the barn after a worship service at sunrise on the hill above.

LIFE AND DEATH

The children were fascinated as they peeked into the cave with the grave clothes visible in candlelight. But their parents and grandparents realized we were celebrating a life-and-death matter: Jesus' death, and our life! When you get down to it, birth and death are two things humanity shares. Death is inevitable. Recently I found a succinct summary for everyone's situation and put it on a sticky note on my fridge:

Bottom line, we all face death. We hide from it, avoid it, fear it, joke about it, blow it off, but most of us fear down deep that our sin problem might finally have to be settled.

COVID-19

As I've been writing this, what should be arriving but a pandemic! Who would have thought our whole world could have been stopped in our tracks so suddenly by an invisible enemy? It's as if all of us are being shaken by the napes of our necks. Who could have anticipated that within a couple months our health, jobs, education, recreation, savings, travel, freedom of association—all aspects of normal life—could be destabilized, almost vanish? Whole countries swing in the air like objects hanging unbalanced on a little mobile swirling in a whirlwind.

At the core of the panic is the fear of death. There's nothing like death staring you in the face to get your attention. Nothing like the collapse of health, and the economy that our lives depend on, to cause most people to try any deterrent or to turn themselves over to anyone who offers deliverance—and especially if they have not embraced life's most reliable and proven Deliverer. Recently on the RZIM website I found a quote by Sam Allberry that puts the marvelous reality succinctly:

> If a cure was announced today for COVID-19 that we could all access within 48 hours, think of the hope that would give man. Two thousand years ago, Jesus' resurrection announced something even greater, the defeat of death itself. It gives us a hope like no other.

COV-ID: TWO SYLLABLES FOR OUR TIMES

I resort to "id" in scrabble sometimes. Handy word, id, given to us by psychoanalytic theory, to be differentiated from "ego" and "super-ego." Here is Webster's definition of **id**: "...the completely unconscious source of instinctual psychic energy derived from needs and drives." Our "ids" seem pretty exercised these days. For those who have not discovered, or have actually rejected, the only "blessed hope," pandemic panic is reasonable, even if denied. Down under, it lurks.

But what's the "COV" connection? Jubilee was given to God's **cov**enant people. I think panic might be connected to uncovering who a person has been covenant partners with, especially if it hasn't been the God who made us. How have we been relating to the One who so loved our sinful race as to take our deserved death penalty in order to reconcile us to Himself? That's what "the Good News" is about—rescued sinners calling out to the perishing, "We implore you on Christ's behalf: Be reconciled to God. God made him who had no sin to be sin for us, so that in him we might become the righteousness of God" (II Corinthians 5:20-21).

BUT THE JUBILEE'S CONNECTION?

Jubilee expresses the thrill of restoration; it's the cry of happiness. It represents the joys awaiting those who have trusted their Kinsman Redeemer to assure them they are covered along their pilgrimage. Earthly Jubilees are "dress rehearsals" for God's Jubilee goal. The door we pass through to approach that reality is our death. And why need a person not fear death? Because God tells those who have received His Son that they have already died on the basis of having been united with the Lord Jesus' death, and also (praise God!) with His resurrection. Yes, they have started to live eternally already. And at death, Jesus assures believers, "Because I live, you also will live" (John 14:19).

INTERRUPTION TIME

The pandemic has the marks of total reorganization, somewhat like the recalibration the Jubilee provided. Jubilee could lead to a redemptive and joyful restoration of a faithful society. In that way, the pandemic effect looks like the opposite, since it's tearing everything down. It's kind of like the confusion of tongues at Babel (Genesis 11:1-9), when men were shaking their fists at God and were bent on building a one-world system in rebellion. God stepped in and spread them out, allowing for new and alternate choices to be made.

OLD TESTAMENT RECALIBRATIONS KEPT HAPPENING

Some two hundred years after the kingdom's high point during the reign of King David, Israel had drifted into idolatry again. God sent the prophet Isaiah to speak to Judah and Jerusalem during four kingships. The book of Isaiah both thunders with warnings of judgment, and rings with songs of restoration. In those days, feasts were being celebrated, but in adulterated and insincere ways—their own ways—not really keeping feasts "unto the LORD." Hear God's assessment of "your feasts, not mine":

> When you come to appear before me, who has asked this of you, this trampling of my courts? Stop bringing meaningless offerings! Your incense is detestable to me. New Moons, Sabbaths and convocations—I cannot bear your evil assemblies. Your New Moon festivals and your appointed feasts my soul hates. They have become a burden to me; I am weary of bearing them (Isaiah 1:12-14).

Isaiah pours out God's warnings and predicts oncoming judgment—which does finally materialize about 100 years later in the fall of Jerusalem in 587 BC. That catastrophe sent Judah to Babylon for 70 years of discipline and repayment of their 490 years of disobeying His command to leave the land fallow the 7th year. Yet Isaiah's message always held out hope for restoration. Let's look once more at this beautiful passage where we can hear the God who never breaks covenant using Jubilee language:

> In the time of my favor, I will answer you, and in the day of salvation I will help you; I will keep you and will make you to be a covenant for the people, to restore the land and to reassign its desolate inheritances, to say to the captives, "Come out," and to those in darkness, "Be free!" (Isaiah 49:8-9).

Yes, He brought them back to His land again, and reorganized them under Ezra and Nehemiah. Their worship of idols seemed cured, but no further word from the Lord came from prophets during the following 400 years before the Incarnation.

THE INCARNATION'S RECALIBRATION

Spiritual compromise, empty worship, and hypocritical leadership had become the order of the day by the time the Father sent the Son into the world. Jesus made His mission clear: "I did not come to judge the world, but to save it" (John 12:47).

Remember that the day Jesus was rejected at Nazareth (Luke 4:14-30), He had announced His redeeming purpose by applying Isaiah's prophecy to Himself:

> The spirit of the Sovereign LORD is on me, because the LORD has anointed me to preach good news to the

poor. He has sent me to bind up the brokenhearted, to proclaim freedom for the captives and release from darkness for the prisoners, to proclaim the year of the LORD'S favor.... (Isaiah 61:1-2).

In the end, Jesus' sinless life, sacrificial death, and resurrection from the dead would so recalibrate the world as to become the calendar's dividing line between "before" and "after"—BC and AD. He left earth, promising a final recalibration, an apocalyptic one, the timing of which He said was known only to the Father.

SIGNALS OF RECALIBRATION TODAY?

Because our current plague harks back to scenes of judgment in biblical times, and because the book of Revelation pictures plagues in the end times, people wonder what today's apocalyptic-scope pandemic is meant to signal or teach us. These questions loom in thinking people's psyche, our "id." It makes us wonder how God views our world today. The Jubilee system might serve as a measuring stick.

COMPARISONS AND CONTRASTS

It would be worth it to look at today's culture through the Jubilee lens, noticing contrasts between the divinely prescribed pattern and the situations that presently blight us. Let's compare.

➢ Our Creator's Jubilee pattern corrected separations and social evils built up over 50-year spans.

   o Our culture's separations and social evils have been building up for ages.

➢ God's pattern brought everyone back gratefully to their family, to their inherited home.

- ○ Suddenly, the pandemic requires all to stay home, but this unearths our culture's digital loneliness, and highlights stresses endemic to broken families.

➢ Land and ownership values were calculated in relationship to their closeness to the 50th year.

- ○ Our housing inequities loom disturbingly in society's face.
- ○ Our economy just borrows, prints more money, and passes on debt indefinitely.

➢ God's pattern interrupted serfdom and slavery, and demanded that the oppressed be released.

- ○ Suddenly, with the pandemic, both employers and employees are in confusion.
- ○ Generational poverty and injustice to daily laborers looms in the face of the wealthy.
- ○ Politicians propose how to redistribute wealth, and economic empires are crumbling.

➢ God's pattern cancelled all built-up economic debt.

- ○ People's savings and job security are being threatened or are already lost.
- ○ Huge national debt threatens our country, families, and individuals with a day of reckoning.

➤ Family deliverance depended on uninterrupted succession of sons as kinsman redeemers.

○ Our families are being obliterated by divorce, cohabitation, and gender reclassification.

○ Our sons and daughters are being slaughtered before they are born.

➤ The Creator kept reminding Israel that their land and their very selves belonged to Him.

○ Secular culture assumes we belong to ourselves, create ourselves, "find" ourselves.

○ With God pronounced "dead," government is expected to take over the role of God.

➤ Along with every warning, God asked for repentance and promised forgiveness and restoration.

○ In secular culture, "sin" is a forbidden concept; thus, repentance becomes unnecessary.

○ The need for forgiveness is avoided; the offer of restoration is mocked or ignored.

➤ When the chosen people ignored God's provision of redemption, judgment was inevitable.

○ Might God be giving the world a judgment warning?

○ Might COVID-19 be foreshadowing our un-dealt-with sin, and our untrusted Redeemer?

To summarize the above, the pandemic is unearthing tell-tale evidences of how seriously our culture is deviating from God's good guidance. Isaiah's chapter 58 powerfully states God's diagnosis of rebellious humanity and hypocritical religion, compared with His own cry for justice and compassion. "'For my thoughts are not your thoughts, neither are your ways my ways,' declares the LORD" (Isaiah 55:8).

IT'S ALL BEEN TAKEN CARE OF!

The Jubilee pattern comes from Israel's early covenant with the LORD. He had delivered them out of slavery and was guiding them to a new home. Centuries later, the foreshadowed Kinsman Redeemer came to earth and paid the redemption price that can forgive our debt of sin. He did this not just for the original Messianic community, but also to bring the whole Gentile world Home as well. He has provided for release from all our bondages. He tells us, "I am the way to the Father" (John 14:6). There is no need for anyone to perish!

We're warned in Scripture that this marvelous cure for the universal plague God calls "sin" will be scoffed at and rejected. Yet, God's Word keeps repeating until the very end, time's end, and our very end, the same good news: "He is patient with you, not wanting anyone to perish, but everyone to come to repentance" (II Peter 3:9). Our Kinsman Redeemer loves us, His beloved, that much. Who will love Him back?

10 ENTER COVID-19:
"Dress rehearsal"?
Facing the inevitability of judgment.

✎ From Isaiah 1:12-14, in response to Israel's feast-keeping in Isaiah's time, what was God's diagnosis, His attitude, and His command?

✎ Comparing God's feast-pattern of societal restorations (focus of Chapter 4) with our post-Christian culture today, how do you think He might be seeing our generation's society?

✎ What sort of message from the Creator do you think we might be getting from the pandemic?

Chapter 11

ALIEN

While writing this during massive human displacement over the world, and at the onset of the Coronavirus saga, I noticed an intriguing detail in the Jubilee stipulations: God's relationship to aliens. He reminds the Israelites of perhaps a foreign thought to us, that "the land must not be sold permanently, because the land is mine and you are but aliens and my tenants" (Leviticus 25:23). In God's sight, the Israelites were aliens in His land!

Furthermore, He commands them to provide for the redemption of non-Israelite aliens living in the land He's given to Israel. (See Leviticus 25:47.) One of the laws He gives them is that when harvesting grain, the edges of the field must be left for the poor and aliens to glean. (See Leviticus 19:9 and 23:22.) If they question the LORD, He reminds them, "Do not mistreat an alien, or oppress him, for you were aliens in Egypt" (Exodus 22:21). It is this rule that allowed Ruth, the Moabite, to glean behind Boaz' harvesters (Ruth 2:2).

ALIEN-NATION

One of my early brushes with the suffering of aliens came in East Africa, seeing desperate Ugandan refugees walking the streets of Nairobi in 1977. Ethnic and religious conflicts in East Africa deposit aliens into each other's nations repeatedly, fleeing for their lives. When the Marxist revolution spun us out of Ethiopia into Kenya, we became aliens too, on the streets of Nairobi. After seven lingering months waiting for visas to Sudan to be granted, we were allowed to serve for the next two years in southern Sudan, reopening two mission hospitals after the North/South civil war. Living for the first time in a Muslim country, we became aliens again. When we returned to America two years later, in some ways we felt like aliens even in our home country.

ENCOUNTERING A SUDANESE ALIEN IN ETHIOPIA

The Marxist government in Ethiopia denied work permits and resident visas to Americans. While back in the States in the 1980s, the Lord led Charlie to our university's Student Health Center, a rare doctor's position that would allow him summers away. He found he could quietly slip into East Africa on three-month visitor visas. He headed to wherever Ethiopians were refugees or in famine. One summer he connected with Ethiopian refugees in Somalia, another two summers in Sudan, and twice he was able to serve in Ethiopia itself. During the summer of 1988, when I was able to join him in Ethiopia, we had a brush with an alien brother's experience that has never left me. We were blessed to be allowed into a clandestine meeting between a group of Ethiopian church elders and a Sudanese visitor named Timothy who had appeared at the mission headquarters in Addis Ababa. Perhaps few Christians in today's world have suffered as much as the Sudanese. Timothy's Uduk ethnic group in Southern Sudan had been attacked by genocidal-breathing Muslim northerners some years before, while he was away on business. His Uduk villagers had fled eastward across the border into Ethiopia and finally straggled into a refugee camp. Pastor Timothy had not seen his dear ones for years, and was trying to reach their missing community languishing among thousands of refugees out on the Ethiopia/Sudan border.

Timothy listened sympathetically to reports of what his Ethiopian brothers had been suffering under communism. When the coffee-with-cream-complexioned Ethiopian brothers finally gave Timothy the floor that memorable day, the small, very dark-skinned brother in the Lord shyly rose to speak. Before sharing his story with them, he chose to read a scripture that was also near to the hearts of Ethiopian Christians while they were facing their Marxist ordeal. Ethiopians had heard little news of Sudanese sufferings. Having lived in Sudan for two years a decade before, Charlie and I could read between the lines as Timothy slowly read from the opening verses of I Peter. My heart was stabbed as I tried to put myself in his shoes. Imagine what each line of these promises meant to Timothy in his personal suffering, and to the persecuted community he led:

Praise be to the God and Father of our Lord Jesus Christ!

In his great mercy he has given us new birth into a living hope through the resurrection of Jesus Christ from the dead

into an inheritance that can never perish, spoil or fade— kept in heaven for you,

who through faith are shielded by God's power until the coming of the salvation that is ready to be revealed in the last time.

In this you greatly rejoice, though now for a little while you may have had to suffer grief in all kinds of trials.

These have come so that your faith—of greater worth than gold, which perishes even though refined by fire—

*may be proved genuine and may result in praise, glory and
honor when Jesus Christ is revealed.*

Though you have not seen him, you love him;

*and even though you do not see him now, you believe in him
and are filled with an inexpressible and glorious joy,*

*for you are receiving the goal of your faith, the salvation of
your souls.*
(I Peter 1:3-9)

Laying his Bible aside, Timothy poured out his Sudanese
believers' struggles under militant Islam. The elders' own experiences with war, hunger, separation, and death caused them to
read between the lines of Timothy's trials and identify deeply.
The cultural and racial barriers evaporated into fervent prayer.
They wept. Later, Timothy was helped to find his community
living in alienation.

WE TOO

When thinking back to that moment, I notice that Peter's
first letter begins with, "To God's elect, <u>strangers</u> in the world,
scattered throughout Pontus, Galatia, Cappadocia...." Peter is
writing to suffering aliens in the first century, seen as foreigners
by their communities. Actually, we who love the Lord Jesus are
all aliens whenever and wherever we live in this fallen world.

THE ADOPTION OPTION

Our identity ultimately depends on which ruler a person
has chosen to give deepest allegiance—our ethnic citizenship,
or to the Lion of Judah (Revelation 5:5). For those who are not
ethnically "of Judah," there is a solution to their alien status. The
Good News announced a new status to Gentiles who believe:

...remember that at that time you were separate from
Christ, excluded from citizenship in Israel and foreigners to

the covenants of the promise, without hope and without God in the world. But now in Christ Jesus you who once were far away have been brought near by the blood of Christ (Ephesians 2:12-13).

Therefore, those who are foreigners to Israel can receive adoption into the Kingdom family. Jesus' offer of redemption for anyone who receives Him brings even Gentiles into His covenant community. As the Scripture explains:

"His purpose was to create in himself one new man out of the two, thus making peace, and in this one body to reconcile both of them to God through the cross" (Ephesians 2:15-16).

WOULD-BE GODS

In the biblical account of the fall, Genesis tells us where, when, and how human rebellion began. Satan insinuated that God was a liar holding out on the human race's first parents: "You will not surely die.... For God knows that when you eat of it your eyes will be opened, and you will be like God, knowing good and evil" (Genesis 3:4-6). Whether thinking of Ethiopia's and Sudan's rulers in the 1980s, or dictators in past ages, or totalitarian regimes today, underneath their despotism lies a desire to be like God to some segment of humanity.

What about democracies? Although immigrants to the New World have avoided some freedom from despotism, we appear to be slipping into careless dismissal of the God of Abraham, Isaac, and Jacob. We too go after false gods, false promises, and false deliverers. Even in supposedly Christianized America, major political parties are promoting child sacrifice, a horrific practice that harkens back to "Baal worship" in biblical times. Our own nation's alienation from the God of our forefathers leaves some citizens of our homeland feeling like aliens, without having gone abroad.

CITIZENSHIP IN THE KINGDOM

In the world, we who know Jesus also know we are aliens. We have chosen to accept the Son's atonement, which happily puts us on the road to the Jubilee. We belong to another Kingdom, honor new patriarchs of the faith, speak a new "language," go by a different Guidebook, appreciate God's feast days, and look forward to a whole new denouement at the King's return. When we've given allegiance to this other King, we inherit a new family, have new goals, expectations, and destiny. How wonderful to know that God accounted for the redemption of aliens even in Moses' day! How great to know that those who long for life with their Father will finally be brought into His house of joy, no longer aliens, at last really Home.

THREATS OF THE ENEMY'S RECALIBRATIONS OF SOCIETY

Along with all these great Kingdom expectations, believers also know they are bi-cultural, having citizenship both on earth and in heaven. The Coronavirus turn of events has suddenly plunged people worldwide into a new level of uncertainty. The pandemic's vast damages may lead to retaliation against an assortment of "candidates for blaming." The western world especially needs to remember centuries of blaming that climaxed in the Holocaust. Incredibly, even before the virus, anti-Semitism's irrational hatred for a tiny nation the size of New Jersey has been rising again. The Scriptures uncover the underlying reason:

When the dragon saw that he had been hurled to the earth, he pursued the woman who had given birth to the male child....Then the dragon was enraged at the woman and went off to make war against the rest of her offspring—those who obey God's commandments and hold to the testimony of Jesus (Revelation 12:13-17).

The internet is making it possible to contact, unite, and in many ways control practically the whole world. Universal fear of death in the pandemic could make people willing to accept some type of global rule, perhaps introduced by the mechanism of enforced global vaccination. Today's technology is already making use of digital chips in animals. If the world becomes increasingly chaotic, a charismatic pretender to God's throne who promises to fix the world just might be welcomed, but at the cost of civil freedoms.

ALIEN CIVILIZATIONS IN C. S. LEWIS' TRUTHFUL FICTION

While required by the pandemic to "shelter at home" during this project's writing, at the end of each day's serious work and the discouragements of the 6:00 news, I've been re-reading C.S. Lewis' Narnia series at bedtime for a bit of pleasurable relief. Lewis' creative land of Narnia frames the metanarrative of the biblical Lion of Judah in delightful, whimsical, philosophical, and deeply theological ways. Adults can learn much from the stories, although the magical adventures feature children from London who are transported into alien territories—into age after age, country after country, island after island. Each tale introduces a new arena of tension between Aslan the Lion (Christ) and the Witch (Satan). She represents evil and recalibrates culture after culture destructively by bringing it to ruin and locking its creatures into stone or some other aberration. Beloved Aslan pays the price of redemption, and brings restoration.

One night, having come to the seventh and last book in the series, *The Last Battle,* I was not so cheered at this point in the near-closure of the wonderful Narnia stories. The blessed land of Narnia is being deceived by an imposter, and is under successful siege by evil invaders, the Calormenes. Jill asks, "Oh Jewel—wouldn't it be lovely if Narnia just went on and on—like what you said it has been"? "Nay, sister," answered Jewel, "all worlds draw to an end; except Aslan's own country." Those who love Aslan and know the book of Revelation can notice clues that parallel our own times. We wish our world would not have to draw to an end, yet as it is, lying under the Witch's spell so to speak, getting to go to Aslan's country would be a wonderful recalibration.

RESTRUCTURING ELEMENTS: IN NARNIA...IN ISRAEL...AND NOW

Leaving the fictional land of Narnia, my mind goes back to the biblical system that climaxed in the Jubilee. Trying to walk in the sandals of the Hebrew community in another age, we can recognize that they were dealing with the same life elements that every society shares. Consider that the darkest time in each fifty-year cycle would have been on the cusp of the Jubilee. That would have been when the society's brokenness and injustices would have compounded to the point that the landless would have become the most hopeless, aliens most neglected, hired laborers and slaves most exhausted, and the homeless most desperate. Moving to our own generation, what mechanisms for correcting societal ills like Israel's do we see in our generation?

VARIOUS FORMS OF CULTURAL RECALIBRATION

The British gentlemen's lectures (mentioned in chapter 1), which started me thinking about the Jubilee's form of recalibration, probably found little acceptance in Kenya half a century ago. All over the world, ethnic jealousies tend to force change by assassinations, coups, and wars. One oppressor overcomes another. When European colonists came to the New World, ethnic groups from various nations agreed to accept each other and experiment with biblically-inspired principles. Leadership change through elections without war has largely kept the peace. In the States, three branches of government written into our Constitution reflect recognition of the human tendency to seize power. But commitment to those founding principles is slipping away, because commitment to the Giver of the principles is slipping away. Even in America, the two covenant communities, both Jews and Christians, are growingly resented as aliens by unbelieving secular society. Peter warns first century Christians (and us as well):

Dear friends, do not be surprised at the painful trial you are suffering, as though something strange were happening to you. But rejoice that you participate in the sufferings of Christ, so that you may be overjoyed when his glory is revealed" (I Peter 4:12-13).

Only those who love Him can rejoice when entering into the Savior's sufferings in some way. Only those who bow to the world's rightful King will be overjoyed when His glory is revealed at His coming.

REMEMBERING ETHIOPIA'S PAINFUL RECALIBRATION

Looking back at how the Ethiopian believers were strengthened during Marxism, I am encouraged to trust God to see His people through any season of living as aliens in a totalitarian milieu. Ethiopia's experiment with communism brought in an influx of Chinese, Russian, and Cuban operatives. The ancient nation suddenly took on a new character. A gleaming emblem of the Red Star was raised high on a main thoroughfare of Addis Ababa. The capitol's venerable old *Muskel* Square was renamed "Red Square." (*Muskel* means cross in Ethiopia's Amharic language—Jesus' cross). Huge billboard faces of three aliens, Marx, Lenin, and Engels, looked down on the old parade grounds where thousands of demonstrators were ordered to line up, or be punished. Centuries-old Ethiopian greetings that included the name of God were forbidden. Left fists must be raised, slogans chanted, allegiance demanded. How could this have happened so suddenly to a country steeped in centuries of Christian history?

When the Revolution's nightmare came to an end, Charlie and I were blessed to get two more years in Ethiopia. The nearest thing to feeling like a Jubilee that I have experienced was an incredible night in the main stadium in Addis Ababa in 1995. With the underground church finally released into the open and found to be greatly multiplied, thousands from all denominations packed the bleachers. Choirs from hundreds of churches sang to their Lord together. Ethiopia was free to praise God again!

MEETING SURVIVORS OF THE REVOLUTION

During those two years back in Ethiopia, I helped our mission's former East African director, John Cumbers, produce a book recording Ethiopian believers' experiences during the Revolution. My follow-up process included the privilege of interviewing over a hundred Christian brothers and sisters. During their testing time, the church had been purified, strengthened, and greatly multiplied. By God's grace, those who relied on their Lord became "overcomers"—the kind of disciples Jesus had urged His people to be in His letters to the seven churches in Asia. (See Revelation 2 and 3.) Those I interviewed testified over and over that during that difficult time, they discovered a deeper life with their suffering Savior which they would not want to have missed. We went to leaders of the Ethiopian evangelical community to ask what title they would want to give to this book recording their testimonies. After taking the matter under consideration, their decision surprised us. "Call it *Count It All Joy*"!

Believers in Ethiopia who survived persecution came to call the fruit of their trial "joy." Faithful Christians who died during the terrors of the Revolution could count it joy as well. Some had assured their executioners of a reality and an invitation for them to consider: "Killing me will issue me into my Savior's joyful presence."

THE END OF THE STORY

Considering the universal subject of death, it is natural that C. S. Lewis (also author of the classic apologetic, *Mere Christianity*) would deal with the issue of death before he finished Narnia's "children's stories." The seventh book is called *The Last Battle,* and it mirrors the book of Revelation. In the final chapter, the children, whose adventures have taken them to many lands and civilizations, leave the "Shadow-lands" (earth) and find themselves to have arrived "further up and further in" (heaven). On the last page, C. S. Lewis assures the reader that, metaphorically, all that had come before would pale in light of what was ahead for the children—and for all of us who have loved the Christ that Aslan represented. The author's last paragraph reveals "the end of the story" to actually be its beginning:

> And for us this is the end of all the stories, and we can most truly say that they all lived happily ever after. But for them it was only the beginning of the real story. All their life in this world and all their adventures in Narnia had only been the cover and the title page: now at last they were beginning Chapter One of the Great Story, which no one on earth has read: which goes on forever: in which every chapter is better than the one before.

This imagined glimpse has long nourished my anticipation of delight in Aslan's land! I've so wished every son of Adam and daughter of Eve would trust "Aslan's" merciful invitation into adventures ahead in His country. Lewis' characters always have two responses, either to be embracers of Aslan, or rejecters. For those who awakened to His love, their alienation from Aslan and his Kingdom was over. They could go on into eternity with joy and anticipation of further adventures with the Lord Jesus, alias Aslan.

GOD'S SOLUTION TO OUR ALIENATION

In the final analysis, we are all aliens on earth, awaiting restoration in the Home of our Creator. Life on earth has many joys, but also "many dangers, toils, and snares," as John Newton's "Amazing Grace" words it. The deepest human pain is actually soul pain, the pain of separation from God. Humans made in His image suffer from an inherent sense of spiritual alienation. God has made every effort to relieve that pain— by settling our sin debt and drawing us to Himself during our sojourn on earth, and on into eternity. Scripture puts His heart and His ultimate promise so very simply in John 3:16: "God so loved the world that he gave his one and only son, that whoever believes in him shall not perish but have eternal life."

11 ALIEN: God's provision for aliens and the blessing of adoption

✎ God reveals key facts about just who are foreigners in His sight (Leviticus 25:23), and also how aliens in the Hebrew's sight were to be treated. How many times are "foreigners" mentioned in Leviticus 25:23-55?

✎ As Ephesians 2:12-13 explains, Gentiles, although excluded from the Chosen People, could be adopted into the Covenant family through Christ's atonement. Do you consider yourself to be a natural Jew, an adopted foreigner, or a continuing foreigner?

✎ How have you experienced the sense of alienation in unfamiliar cultures, or within your own? Where or when do you expect to feel truly "at home"?

Chapter 12

SOON

Good Friday is always such a bad Friday for those of us who realize what that day cost our Kinsman Redeemer, for our "good." Saturday comes as a relief; and Sunday, of course, Jesus' resurrection celebration! This year was unique, too, with COVID-19's deaths emphasizing the whole world's need for a Savior.

A blessed break in our family's pandemic lockdown came on Saturday. Our son, Nat, and his wife and their son and I decided to walk in the cool of the evening down to our nearby Kitten Creek, where it flows under the lane's low concrete bridge. As we were strolling eastward toward the crossing, a huge white thunderhead moved in above it, low on the horizon ahead of us. The billowing clouds glistened unbelievably white, then became tinged with gold. Soon the gold tints turned pink as the sunset cast its reflections from the west. What a gift to us to just happen to be there the only five minutes this epiphany could be experienced! It took my breath away. *Yes, yes,* I thought, *the heavens declare the glory of God; the skies proclaim the work of his hands* (Psalm 19:1). *How could anyone see this,* I mused, *and not be given hope that there's a better world to know?*

At that little grotto, trees lining the stream were leafing out in various shades of green—elms, hackberries, oaks, walnuts, and mulberries below the majestic old sycamores and cottonwoods. I noticed my first violet in the grass, and the scent of Sweet William made me scan the undergrowth for those lovely blue wildflowers. Memories generated there flowed back—a sod-home a teenager built into the bank, camping overnights, Fourth of July picnics, *Tashlich* stones thrown into the creek—God's good gifts, all.

SUNSETS

According to Hebrew time, a day begins not at sunrise, but at sunset. This little walk we took was a substitute for Grandpa's sunset ritual, now that we are missing him so. Charlie's ritual? The grandkids would pile into the bed of his old Ford truck, and we'd drive north a couple miles to a high pasture across from a pond we named "Baby Bishoftu"—reminiscent of a beloved crater lake in Ethiopia, but 1/100th of its size. If we got there early, Charlie would have all of us laughing as he mimicked bull noises and got a row of cows to gather at the fence in response to his bellows. If the resident bull got mad enough to paw the ground, Charlie would be satisfied. The kids would walk their beloved dog, Sheba. We'd all watch for the sun's moment of setting, sing a hymn, say a prayer, and drive home heart warmed. Home, family, land, freedom, assurance of redemption, expectation—they were all wrapped up in Charlie's rituals, touches of Jubilee-type goodness.

COMING TO OUR CONCLUSION

Dear Reader, as we come to the close of this time spent together, I've been amazed at the wealth mined just out of the Jubilee, just one slender vein of Scripture. The Word of God is so pregnant with life, so demonstrative of truth, that it awes the mind, the heart, and the spirit.

When I started writing this study, my original hope was just to draw our attention to what God reveals in His Jubilee patterns—wisdom and principles that are valuable even for our lives today. Most of us are given a few years of maturity in which to respond, and thereby flourish in relationships and grow in spirit. However, the pandemic turned my thinking more to life's final issues. The Jubilee progression can provide a set of "dress rehearsals" before the curtain on eternity actually rises.

MINING

Furthermore, Jubilee gives us a metaphor for all history. We can make a search through the Word using the Jubilee context as sort of a magnet picking up filings that cling. Those valuable cross reference listings in study Bibles expand and confirm a passage being considered. Only the earnest believer takes time to go mining. But those who invest in deep examination discover that God's Word to man proves itself by its continuity and its unity. That is why so many skeptics who have set out to disprove the Bible (which necessitates going over it) in the end have come to believe, and to do so firmly—so firmly as to become outstanding advocates and apologists for God's truth.

CONTINUITY AND UNITY

In the Jubilee vein, we can mine out the continuity of the family through whom God chose to demonstrate His message to the world. A search through the cross references from Genesis to Revelation has led us to Jubilee ties: first as given to Moses in the Torah; then to its relevance to the book of Ruth, set in Bethlehem, when Naomi's kinsman redeemer eventually became the ancestor of King David. Moving on through I Samuel, David was a shepherd boy in Bethlehem who his father Jesse had to call out from the fold to let Samuel anoint the youngest son to be Israel's new king. That leads us to the New Testament's genealogy list in Matthew 1 – Boaz to Obed, Obed to Jesse, Jesse to David. We can continue in the Gospels, with Jesus being born in Bethlehem. And that leads us to wondering why Bethlehem has been the scene of all this Messianic foreshadowing.

BETHLEHEM?

What was this town? Messianic rabbi Jonathan Cahn's *The Book of Mysteries* includes a related meditation. He explains that Bethlehem was the sheepfold town where animals were set apart for sacrifices at the Temple in nearby Jerusalem. Oh my, how significant for the Lamb of God to be born there, and for Temple shepherds to be the first messengers of the birth of the royal Son of David! How mindlessly we sometimes parrot the Christmas story: "So, Joseph went up from the town of Nazareth in Galilee to Judea, to Bethlehem the town of David, because he belonged to the line of David...." (Luke 2:4).

And when the family line of David finally comes to its conclusion in the last book of the Bible, the Messianic King— "the Lion of Judah"—appears. He is the only one worthy to open the scroll that reveals the future. (See Revelation 5:5.) And in Revelation's last chapter, what were the last words of the Lamb-become-Lion? "I am the Root and Offspring of David, and the bright Morning Star" (Revelation 22:16). In those two titles, we hear identity-confirming code words that picture themes that throb throughout God's message: Jesus' covenant family continuity, and eternity's new day dawning!

WIDENING OUT

As our magnet picks up filings across this biblical panorama from Genesis to Revelation, we find continuity throughout the book, even though it was recorded by many writers and over centuries. We can go back and forth from the first to the last book, seeing their relationships. We see the first Adam, and then the second Adam. We see Eve, and then the Bride of the second Adam. We see God's unfaithful wife, and hear His New Covenant promise to finally restore her to Himself. We see Eden at the beginning and then a new heaven and earth at the end. As the book of Revelation closes, again we find Eden's tree of life, the river of life, and a new unspoiled Jerusalem. Light from Father and Son are so glorious that the sun is unneeded.

THE WEDDING IN HIS HEART

The book of Revelation has many chapters predicting judgments, but to what resolution does the biblical drama come? The climax is initiated by a wedding! Dragging our magnet back through the Old Testament, we pick up marriage metaphors starting with the first couple in Eden, then the Hebrew family being brought into covenant relationship with God. Israel is called His "wife." In the New Testament, however, believers are called the "bride"—the "bride in waiting."

While He was on earth, Jesus' parables hinted about His wedding. The parable of the king's son's wedding in Matthew 22 reveals that the Bridegroom expects to be rejected by His chosen people. The parable of the ten virgins waiting for the bridegroom's arrival in Matthew 25:1-13 warns that only those truly born of the Spirit will be allowed to enter the wedding. Five had oil, symbol of the Holy Spirit, and five did not. Every generation of Spirit-filled "virgins" has hoped Jesus would come at their generation's midnight.

WHAT TO EXPECT

As He warned, those expecting His return would be scoffed at. (See II Peter 3:3.) The world would not understand that the Father waits ever so patiently, "not wanting anyone to perish, but everyone to come to repentance" (II Peter 3:9). Most of today's world continues in general rebellion against the Creator, and even some Christians scoff at interest in His return. During the Incarnation, the religious establishment rejected the Lord, and many religious people today label those who talk about the Lord's second coming as "fanatics." Yet God's promise is that the trumpet will finally sound. Jesus predicted a sobering aspect of His return: "At that time the sign of the Son of Man will appear in the sky, and all the nations of the earth will mourn" (Matthew 24:30). Why "mourn"? His coming will be a shocking and convicting revelation to His rejectors. And David's house?

Zechariah predicts Israel's reaction poignantly:

> And I will pour out on the house of David and the inhabitants of Jerusalem a spirit of grace and supplication. They will look on me, the one they have pierced, and they will mourn for him as one mourns for an only child, and grieve bitterly for him, as one grieves for a firstborn son (Zechariah 12:10).

BIBLICAL AUTHENTICATION OF THE LAMB

Had this "firstborn son's" identity not been revealed? The Messianic Son was born in Bethlehem, close to where He would eventually die. Just a few miles north of His birthplace, the prefigured sacrificial Lamb's blood was shed thirty-three years later for the remission of sins. Exactly when? At the hour when lambs had died at the time of the evening sacrifice, on the precise day of the Passover Feast. The Savior rose from death on the precise day of the Feast of First Fruits. These continuities in history and in prophetic revelation can only be attributed to God. The Bible wasn't written by one author with an agenda. Actually, from another standpoint, the Scriptures' writers were all inspired by one Person, the Spirit of God. (See II Peter 1:20-21.) The Spirit's purpose was to bring readers to faith in the central character of the Scriptures, the Redeemer.

BUT HOW ABOUT US?

So, what does all this have to do with us today? Well, to begin with, the Apostle John is frank to tell readers the intention of his Gospel's account: "Jesus did many other miraculous signs which are not recorded in this book. But these are written that you may believe that Jesus is the Christ, the Son of God, and that by believing you may *have life* in his name" (John 20:30-31).

➢ At a time when the world's people are frightened by COVID-19, *having life* surely sounds like a welcome assurance, whether the virus infects us or not.

➢ At a time when even the secular world is calling today's events "apocalyptic," it would be only prudent to consider the reality of judgment, and accept God's provision of forgiveness, even though it would mean admitting the need for a Savior. His sin payment is available to "put to the account" of anyone who trusts Him. As the Urban Alternative's Tony Evans puts it so simply, "God will let you go to heaven on credit, Jesus' credit."

➢ At a time when death keeps being the media's focus, it's good to believe John when he clarifies life and death issues:

> Anyone who does not believe God has made him [God] out to be a liar, because he has not believed the testimony God has given about His Son. And this is the testimony: God has given us eternal life, and this life is in His Son. He who has the Son has life; he who does not have the Son of God does not have life." (I John 5:10-12)

➢ At a time when most people whose cultures have been given biblical revelation aren't caring to attend the "imagined wedding," it would be wise to awaken to the fact that the King's love is real and desirable, and to reconsider His invitation.

➢ At a time when those who have received the Savior are facing a gathering hostile storm, we are encouraged to recognize its deceptive source and to prepare for what global government may mean in terms of enforced obedience to a unified kingdom of this world.

Parallel to all those sorts of considerations, even when signs of the times loom over our skies, we can actually be encouraged by the old saying, "The future is as bright as the promises of God!" The virus may blow over and the pressures may lessen, but urgency of response to the Lover of our souls remains at the point of every person's tension—the responsibility to choose which sovereign we will serve in our earthly time, and therefore, in our eternity.

IN THE MEANTIME

The risen Christ told His people not to fixate on the time of His return, but on their commission to spread the word of His resurrection. His resurrection had become the first-fruit in the harvest of all who would trust Him. While pursuing that end goal, the sons and daughters of the Kingdom are to reflect the King's concerns. The New Testament pulsates with those concerns, undergirded by the Old Testament's revelation of the LORD's heart for the widow and orphan, the poor, the oppressed, the prisoner, and the alien—concerns we are to engage in during our short lifespans.

In the Torah's Jubilee context, taking into account humanity's fallen nature, God's Owner's Manual lays out guidelines as guardrails against human selfishness and greed. Such as? Summarizing stipulations in Leviticus 25: *Don't take advantage of each other, don't charge interest from a brother, don't sell him food at a profit, don't rule over workers ruthlessly, allow a price to be paid to redeem people out of servitude.* And in Deuteronomy 15: "If a fellow Hebrew, a man or a woman sells himself to you and serves you six years, in the seventh year you must let him go free...and not empty-handed. Supply him liberally..." And in Exodus 23: God's basic reminder: "Do not oppress an alien; you yourselves know how it feels to be aliens, because you were aliens in Egypt" (Exodus 23:9). These precepts recognized fallen humanity's propensity to oppress each other. They directed a God-honoring society to treat the needy with kindness, and to release people from servitude and poverty in orderly, lawful ways.

Scriptural guidance on how to live mercifully was all based on the character of God, who says of Himself: "He defends the cause of the fatherless and the widow, and loves the alien, giving him food and clothing" (Deuteronomy 10:18). His basic Ten commandments of the Law were engraved "on stone" slabs. After Pentecost, the Spirit of God would come to write God's precepts "on the hearts" of those who would respond to the love of God and receive His new nature.

In our particular time of history, the sheer magnitude of humanity's buildup of unredeemed societal injustices to the poor, the widow, the orphan, and the alien is staggering. And then in marches the pandemic. It acts to show up these inequalities that are multiplied over the whole world— personal and institutional sins crying out on our TVs, in our own communities, and abroad. The virus humbles humanity. It shows us how vulnerable and powerless and blind and unrighteous we are.

THREE CROWNS: CORONA CROWN, JESUS' THORN CROWN, CROWN OF RIGHTEOUSNESS

The spring of 2020 edition of RZIM's quarterly magazine, "Just Thinking," included an article by John Lennox titled, "Where is God in a Coronavirus World?" This particular virus is named "Corona" because microscopically it resembles a crown. John Lennox reminds us what we can be thankful for:

> Perhaps the coronavirus might function as a huge loudspeaker, reminding us of the ultimate statistic: that one out of every one of us dies. If this induces us to look to the God we may have ignored for years, but who wore a crown of thorns in order to bring us back into relationship with Him and into a new, unfractured world beyond death, then the coronavirus, in spite of the havoc it has wreaked, will have served a very healthy purpose.

The corona crown forebodes sickness and death. But the pandemic's fallout also uncovers aspects of humanity's unrighteousness and our universal spiritual need for the redemption that only the righteous One can provide. His crown of thorns is a symbol of man's perverse attempts to "kill God." Significantly, the blood stains from the Savior's wounded head and hands mirrored the doorframes' blood marks when the blood of the Passover lamb protected the Hebrews from death as they exited bondage into a whole new life.

In contrast, a life-giving crown awaits those who have said "I do" to the Bridegroom, a "crown of righteousness"—Jesus' righteousness—gifted to those who trust Him. His re-appearing will vindicate the One who died wearing the crown of thorns to save His Bride from judgment's eternal death. His resurrection

—gifted to those who trust Him—can change anyone's death into their door to life.

Paul was blinded when He first encountered Jesus on the road to Damascus, but after embracing the Lord, he longed to see Jesus. He encouraged Timothy, with these words:

> I have fought the good fight, I have finished the race, I have kept the faith. Now there is in store <u>a crown of righteousness</u> which the Lord, the righteous judge, will award to me on that day—and not only to me, but to all who have longed for his appearing (II Timothy 4:7-8).

BE ASSURED

Early Christians expected the Lord's return perhaps in their lifetimes. But time marched on, and people died. Paul comforted the Thessalonians about their elders who had gone on before the Lord's return:

> Brothers, we do not want you to be ignorant about those who fall asleep, or to grieve like the rest of men, who have no hope. We believe that Jesus died and rose again and so we believe that God will bring with Jesus those who have fallen asleep. According to the Lord's own word, we tell you that we who are still alive, who are left till the coming of the Lord, will certainly not precede those who have fallen asleep. For the Lord himself will come down from heaven, with a loud command, and with the voice of the archangel and with the trumpet call of God, and the dead in Christ will rise first. After that, we who are still alive and are left will be caught up together with them in the clouds to meet the Lord in the air. And so, we will be with the Lord forever. Therefore, encourage each other with these words (I Thessalonians 4:13-18).

Many generations have been encouraged by this scriptural promise. Yet, the long unfulfilled gap in history makes us wonder. Noticeably, the situation between the Church and Israel is as yet unreconciled, and the testimony has not yet gone fully out to the world. Still, God's promises are sure, and we await fulfillment. But we ponder His mysterious use of His last word to the Bride, "soon."

IMMINENCE

When on earth, the Bridegroom kept telling His Bride-to-be to stay faithful, to keep alert, to warn, win, wait, and watch for Him. He kept telling her to be ready, since He would come unexpectedly, imminently. Imminence means: "ready to take place." His imminent return refers to Jesus' promise to return "soon." Soon on God's calendar and ours may differ. Soon may even depend on His covenant peoples' responses. But soon is an encouragement, a commitment of love, a holding out of hope. In the Bible's last chapter, the Bride and Groom are repeatedly calling back and forth to each other, she calling Him to "come," and He promising, "soon."

"COME, FOR ALL THINGS ARE READY!" (LUKE 14:17)

For years, a framed scene has hung on our dining room wall, the one on the cover of this book. Below the picture are the words from Jesus' parable of the Great Banquet, "Come, for all things are ready." The Host's invited guests rejected Him— made excuses why they hadn't time to come. Our Lord's veiled metaphor reveals that God is so eager to bless and celebrate that He threw open His arms indiscriminately to the needy in the whole town and countryside. What a serendipitous surprise that celebration would have been to the poor, crippled, blind, and lame! Spiritually speaking, that's all of us.

How merciful is His eagerness to walk with His Bride on our earthly jubilee journeys as we joyfully anticipate the approaching Wedding Supper of the Lamb promised in Revelation 19:6-9.

In our fallen world, people do not just "live happily ever after" following each threatening phase of history. But the table for the Wedding Feast is being set (Revelation 19:7). People of every tribe and nation have already gathered (Revelation 7:9-10). The whole world He created is called to come to the King's wedding, and everyone needs to know so. Anyone may choose to live happily ever after, in God's glory. All the returning, redeeming, releasing, and restoring will finally be completed.

Dear Reader, may we meet at the Wedding that brings in the Jubilee!

12 SOON:
Jesus the Bridegroom, believers the Bride

INHERENT IN "BRIDE" IS A PROMISE THAT AWAITS COMPLETION

What do Jesus' parables related to His wedding show you personally?

✎   The wedding of the king's son in Matthew 22:1-10.

✎   The ten virgins waiting for the Bridegroom's arrival in Matthew 25:1-13.

✎   The parable of the great banquet in Luke 14:15-24
    (See also Revelation 7:9; 19:6-9.)

✎   The Bride calls, "Come!" (Revelation 22:17), and longs for His appearing (II Timothy 4:8). How do you think or feel about Jesus' return? Why?

EPILOGUE

WRITTEN ON INDEPENDENCE DAY, 2020

At the end of writing this book, the author finds herself trying to celebrate the 4th of July 2020 in a nation that is largely celebrating independence from the Judeo/Christian God— that is, from any sense of His having created us, holding us accountable, and eventually judging each of us for our response.

THIS IS BECOMING A "PERIOD PIECE."

Writing this book has seemed like taking a short course in change. Starting with the intention of sharing somewhat lighthearted Jubilee gems, its tone has been impacted by the seriousness of the COVID-19 pandemic. Now race riots are upon us. The fabric of our nation appears to be tearing apart. I'm just one small woman without impressive credentials, but at the end of a rather personal story, I can't help wanting to add a few more "epilogue" thoughts. Sorry, dear Reader; I grew up in an "essays in 2,000 words or less" generation.

IIRF BOOK

Two years ago, I was documenting a saga that was eventually published in Germany by the International Institute for Religious Freedom (IIRF). Their associate had asked for my unpublished manuscript because the Institute focuses on growing persecution of Christians in today's world. Actually, I cooperated with updating the project because the resulting book, *Overcomers,* could give voice to testimonies of God's faithfulness to His people during the Marxist Revolution that gripped Ethiopia from the 1970s to the 1990s.

I was glad when it was published a few months later in Oregon, becoming available in America. It probably was catalogued under "Ethiopia," "history," or "persecution." However, I didn't really expect a related and similar scenario to emerge in our own nation, at least not particularly soon. I was wrong.

DÉJÀ VU

On July the 4th of 2020, in today's milieu, I'm having a gnawing sense of déjà vu—having memories of seeing these elements before—in a different context, with variations, but essentially the same. During Ethiopia's Marxist Revolution, similar components quickly tore the nation apart and re-programed the citizenry. Ethiopia hurriedly became a totalitarian state.

Remembering how Marxist methods were implemented in Ethiopia, and seeing similar elements now on native soil, I can't help comparing and contrasting the two situations, the double contexts of my own pilgrimage. Techniques tailored to undo our sophisticated but historically illiterate American society seem basically the same as for the unsuspecting Ethiopians' saga. Fear can recalibrate any society.

Dear Reader, can you understand my sense of apprehension as I share with you some of Ethiopia's experience half a century ago? Basic to radicalization are the mottos, "Divide and conquer!" and "Don't let a crisis go to waste!" In Ethiopia's case the crisis used was a terrible famine; in ours it's the convergence of multiple issues: worldviews, marriage, abortion, gender, race, climate, politics, virus, and more. Groups waiting in the wings with all manner of separate agendas are being given an ideal moment to "divide and conquer."

I wrote down a long list of 20 types of coercion used to quickly recalibrate Ethiopia. After each scenario, I listed comparable elements beginning to appear in our nation today. Here is a general list of what was implemented in Ethiopia. Notice the takeover tools: *propaganda, character assassination of the leaders, fear, disarmament, surveillance, accusation/shaming sessions, forced parading, seizing media, denying assembly, closing churches, silencing God references, confiscating properties, restricting travel, requiring ID documents, brainwashing, persecution, imprisoning, torturing, and executions.*

All these in the name of the recalibration's slogan: "Ethiopia first!" Not the citizenry first, but the nation first. The nation (i.e. her dictators) had replaced God.

[If you would like to see an amplified comparison pdf titled, "20/20 DÉJÀ VU in 2020," comparing what took place in Ethiopa then with what was happening in America in 2020, contact the publisher, olivepressbooks@gmail.com.]

RACE-FOCUSED CONFUSIONS

As this book goes to press, our society is facing facts of chronic injustices and systemic racial suffering. Many are really "hearing" realities long unrecognized. Hopefully, real structural changes may be undertaken. But the movement's aberrations have also gone viral, worldwide. Venom turned loose between groups of people being categorized simply by their skin color is senseless. These polarizations deeply sadden countless people scattered among the various ethnic groups into which we each were born. Assumed solidarity just based on color or sex or political party is a hoax. People of many complexions are earnestly wanting to stand in solidarity with the primary concerns of the movement, and are even willing to peacefully protest in the streets with the black community. Yet marches are often marred by groups with manipulative agendas who use the built-in propaganda opportunity, or are spoiled by those who take advantage of anarchism on the loose.

JUBILEE CONNECTION?

Dear Reader, you may be asking, "Whatever does this situation have to do with the Jubilee?" It might have more relevance than we could at first think. In the preceding chapters, we've explored the prophetic aspect of the feasts. The final seventh (signifying completion) plus one becomes the Jubilee, the goal, the conclusion, the climax, and the reward. Daniel, and other of God's prophets, as well as Jesus Himself, foretold the ultimate conclusion, of which only God knows the timing.

A pre-requisite indicated in the Scriptures was the Jewish presence back in Jerusalem, a reality in place now for 70-some years. Latter-day signs of the times were predicted, nearly all of which are falling into place at this unique time in history, at least in embryo form. They are not just local manifestations. Even the secular press speaks of them using the terms "apocalyptic" and "of biblical proportions." Never have we had such widespread culminating and converging signs on a global level, threatening the whole world's health, economies, national stabilities, and international peace prospects—all based on conflicting worldviews which are increasingly intolerant of each other.

"AS IT WAS IN THE TIME OF NOAH..." (MATTHEW 24:37)

Prophetically, the Bible has warned us that just before our Lord's return, attitudes would be cold toward faith, and relationships would increase in arrogance and brutality. Even Darwin and Sartre had to admit that their secular, godless worldviews would lead to massive violence and bloodshed in our century. Ours has been the bloodiest in history.

Scripture explains that our first ancestors' rebellion brought death into an altogether good world. For those who do not accept God's deliverance, arrogant pride is at the root of spiritual death. Dismissing, ignoring, or defying God cooperates with His enemy. Today, we are seeing deception, confusion, and violence inspired and fanned by the arch Deceiver. He (not the group with whose viewpoint we disagree) is mankind's enemy.

WHO WILL TRUST THE DELIVERER?

None of what is happening in the world is a surprise to God. He's predicted it. He already acted to overcome the world. He wrote down what to expect, so as to prepare those who listen to be forewarned and thus forearmed in the spiritual battle being fought "in the heavenlies" (Ephesians 6:12). Thanks be to the Savior, we can be forgiven of our sins—our selfishness, our pride, our lusts for power, our mistreatments of each other, and our complicity with the enemy in rebellion against our Maker. ["Did God really say...?" Come on Eve, "you will be like God..."] (See Genesis 3:1, 5) Wanting to be our own god is why we all need the Savior the Father sent—no matter on which sides of the growing rifts we find ourselves.

Dear Reader, God longs for us to desire Him and His ways of living on earth, and to eventually enjoy His Homelife in heaven. "No eye has seen, no ear has heard, no mind has conceived what God has prepared for those who love him..." (I Corinthians 2:9). The Lord of glory invites all humanity to choose His provided way of access to all He has in store for us through the atonement He provided. Atonement must come before the Jubilee. God's promises are sure. He invites everyone everywhere to come to Him, to enjoy a whole new life in His recalibrated ultimate Jubilee! Oh, that we might each embrace the reconciliation He longs to bless us with. That will be our deepest joy, and His as well.

ACKNOWLEDGMENTS OF APPRECIATION

DEAR READER, For any who take time to read this page, I'm grateful. Our Wellspring Writers' group's habit is for each member to choose a word for their year. Mine for 2020 was "appreciation." As I think back over creating this year's Jubilee project, it has spanned my life experience, causing me to re-appreciate my own mentors and seasons of development, and many appear in vignette form in this book. My desire to share our own adventures with "Aslan" i.e. Yeshua/Jesus, is undergirded by having met Him, loved Him, and been guided by His Spirit throughout life, and through this latest writing project.

PUBLISHING I am deeply appreciative of the labor of love of two major enablers. It has been the kind editing of Shelly Larkins that enabled the book to be gone over and much improved by her skillful expertise. And it took the acceptance and professional excellence of Cheryl Zehr at Olive Press to bring it to publication. Claire Bishop designed the cover overlaying the Jubilee portrayal, which *Decision* magazine gave permission to use. The insignia on the back cover was kindly created for our 50th anniversary by Ginger Olson. Our local Wellspring Writers' group and Marcia Bascom have given insightful advice. This small book rises out of the loving ministrations and prayers of many, both named and unnamed herein.

VANTAGE POINT It was Jim Rayburn's passion for Jesus that awakened my thirst to know Him. The Bible, His word, is basic to that pursuit. Readers will notice my writing's persistently panoramic paradigm. It was Bess Combs who early in my married life in St. Joseph, Missouri, taught many of us in her women's Bible class to approach every section of Scripture in light of the Bible's entirety. She would put her pen down on a passage and then sweep it like an arc from Genesis to Revelation. I am deeply grateful for what Miss Comb's paradigm transferred to my study and life.

BOOKS My life in the Lord started with the all-surpassing book from God, initially with the first chapter of John's Gospel, as related in this Jubilee book's chapter 5. Books have been my grounding mentors ever since, such as Merrill Tenney's *John: the Gospel of Belief*; Dawson Trotman's *Topical Memory System*; J. B. Phillips' modern translation of the New Testament and his *Your God Is Too Small*; Watchman Nee's *The Normal Christian Life*; Oswald Saunders' *Christ Indwelling and Enthroned*; C.S. Lewis' *Narnia Series*; Dietrich Bonhoeffer's *Life Together*; Francis Schaeffer's *The God Who Is There*; E. Stanley Jones' *The Word Become Flesh*; works of Henri Nouwen; and many more.

LIVES Books bring us into fellowship with writers we may never meet until Glory, but flesh and blood brothers and sisters are our faith's encouragers and sustainers along life's earthly journey. Each of us have a few lifelong friends who bolster our lives and keep us honest over the years. My list of names of those who have shared life and prayed for our family for decades would be exhaustive. My heart overflows with thanksgiving for each dear brother and sister in a blessed multiplicity of communities—home town folks; the Young Life gang; fellow SIM missionaries; national believers in Ethiopia, Sudan, Kenya, Austria, and Romania; our Stateside friends and church fellowships in Kansas City, St. Joe, Troy, Riley, and Manhattan; our local Wellspring Fellowship experimenters and more. Many friends who have not awakened to the Lord Jesus have also played significant roles in my life. And aching for them motivates me to keep trying to present evidence to each, or pray that others more effective than myself will reach their minds and hearts.

THE SPIRIT Of course, my motivation and enablement have been by the Spirit of God who took up residence in me when I trusted Jesus as my only Savior and acknowledged Lord. His presence within me, and shepherding care throughout life, call forth my deepest thankfulness. One of the first verses I counted on as a new believer, Philippians 1:6, has proven true. Yes, "... being confident of this, that he who began a good work in you will carry it on to completion until the day of Christ Jesus."

A WRITER'S CONCERN My father used to tell me, "There are two kinds of people in the world, those who sit, and those who sit and think." God seemed to make me the latter. When I think, my spaghetti thoughts are best untangled by writing them down. When I do, I want to share them somehow, and that leads to pages, and pages can grow into books. Our Lord calls His people to be "watchmen on the wall"—observers, discerners, warners—always looking to Him for His viewpoint. Writing can be a blessing, but it is also dangerous. May He guide, correct, and protect!

FELLOW TRAVELERS My dear husband Charlie often said, "Believers don't need to say 'goodbye,' just 'so long.'" It will be wonderful to meet mutual pilgrims we've not known on earth, and re-engage with those we've loved and been loved by along life's path. Our Lord's promise is sure. He is still coming "soon." We eagerly await entering into His Jubilee's next adventures "further up and further in," as C. S. Lewis pictured it.

ETERNAL HOPE However, for now, life's 2020 saga appears to be bringing us into a time of difficult testing. The Lord has proven Himself to be the sure source of overcoming in every generation. We trust Him to be faithful in this present season of life. Ours is a living, confident, eternal hope shared with the faithful who over the centuries have trusted His promises, and joyfully anticipated His Return.

> Praise be to the God and Father of our Lord Jesus Christ. In his great mercy he has given us new birth into a living hope through the resurrection of Jesus Christ from the dead, and into an inheritance that can never perish, spoil or fade—kept in heaven for you, who through faith are shielded by God's power until the coming of the salvation that is ready to be revealed in the last time. In this you greatly rejoice, though now for a little while you may have had to suffer grief in all kinds of trials (I Peter 1:3-6).

What a marvelous gathering we look forward to when we finally reach Home and come into His inheritance at the ultimate Jubilee! Until then, "So long," beloved readers.

Kay Bascom

OTHER BOOKS BY THE AUTHOR

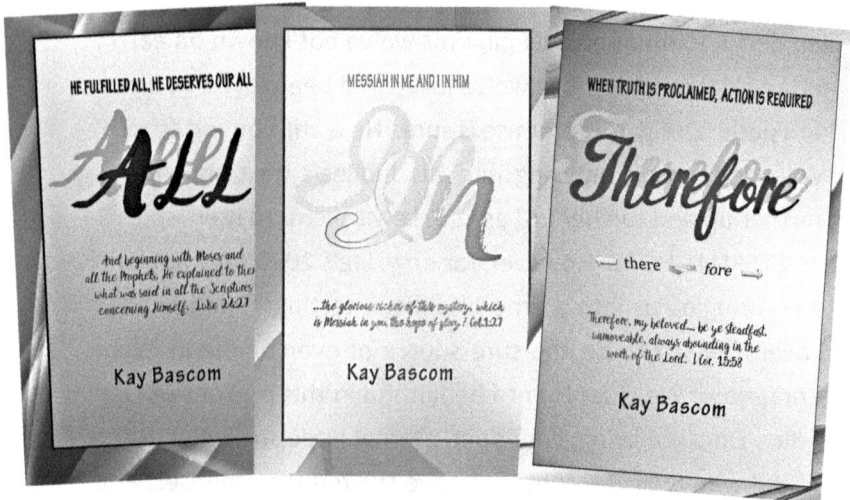

Three 12-week Bible studies that give
insight into Messiah and the Biblical Feasts and
teach us to give Him our all and live in His power.

Overcomers chronicles many evangelicals' testimonies to
God's deliverance during Ethiopia's Marxist Revolution.

The *Overcomers Study Guide* has seven studies related to the
Ethiopian experience then, and applied to believers' situations now.
Supplements A to F supply analyses and resources for
overcoming in our wider world today.

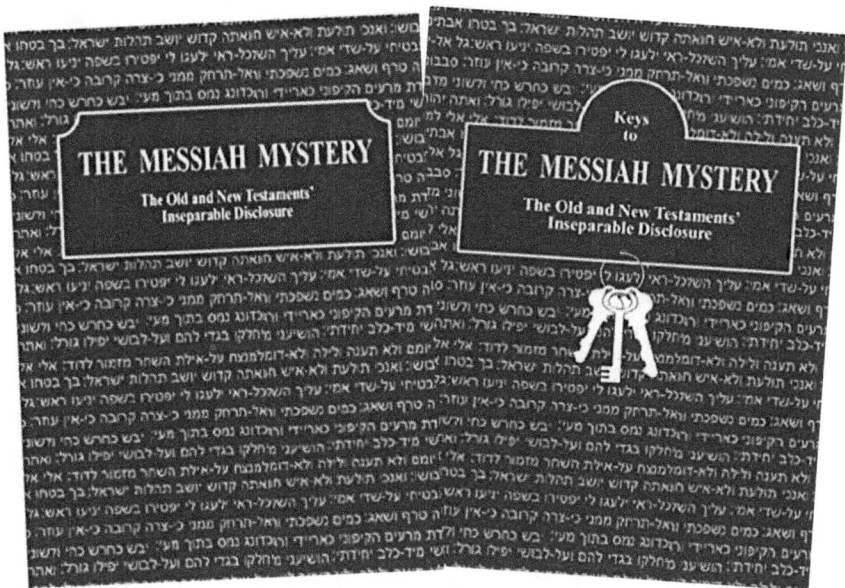

The Messiah Mystery: The Old and New Testaments' Inseparable Disclosure gives readers a thorough look at the panoramic biblical overview of man's pilgrimage on this earth from Creation to Consummation.
Keys to the Messiah Mystery is a study guide.

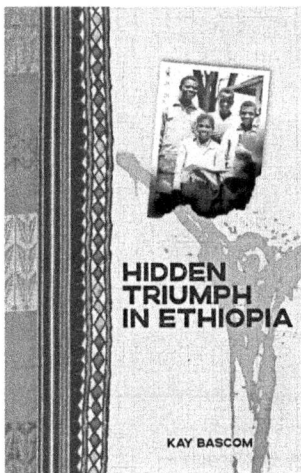

Hidden Triumph in Ethiopia focuses on the representative life of Negussie among his fellow believers' triumph of faith during Ethiopia's Marxist Revolution.